PRODUCT INNOVATION
AND DIRECTIONS
OF INTERNATIONAL TRADE

This is a volume
in the Arno Press collection

MULTINATIONAL CORPORATIONS:
Operations and Finance

Advisory Editor
Stuart Bruchey

See last pages of this volume
for a complete list of titles

PRODUCT INNOVATION
AND DIRECTIONS
OF INTERNATIONAL TRADE

Louis T. Wells, Jr.

ARNO PRESS

A New York Times Company
New York • 1980

Editorial Supervision: Erin Foley

First publication 1980 by Arno Press Inc.

Copyright © 1980 by Louis T. Wells, Jr.

MULTINATIONAL CORPORATIONS: Operations and Finance
ISBN for complete set: 0-405-13350-2
See last pages of this volume for titles.

Manufactured in the United States of America

Library of Congress Cataloging in Publication Data

Wells, Louis T
    Product innovation and directions of international
trade.

    (Multinational corporations)
    Originally presented as the author's thesis, Harvard,
1966.
    Includes bibliographical references.
    1. Product management--Mathematical models.
2. Commercial policy--Mathematical models. I. Title.
II. Series.
HF5415.15.W44   1980   658.5'038   80-602
ISBN 0-405-13392-8

PRODUCT INNOVATION AND DIRECTION OF INTERNATIONAL
TRADE

Louis T. Wells, Jr.

A thesis submitted in partial fulfillment
of the requirements for the degree of
Doctor of Business Administration

Graduate School of Business Administration
George F. Baker Foundation
Harvard University
June 1966

SUMMARY

The businessman is faced with ever-changing opportunities and threats from international trade. To prosper, he must be able to make sense out of these trade flows in order that he can take advantage of export markets when they exist and so that he may take appropriate action when import competition threatens.

The economists have offered various models to conceptualize these trade flows. Adapting some of these models to the particular characteristics of consumer durables produces a description of a trade cycle. When a new, high-income product is introduced, it is likely to be manufactured first in the United States, where the largest high-income market exists. If scale-economies are significant, a United States producer may have lower costs than a potential foreign producer manufacturing only for his smaller market. Hence, the United States may successfully export the product. However, as demand increases in other countries, foreign competition is likely to start. When a foreign market is large enough, lower factor costs may enable a manufacturer overseas to produce more cheaply than a U. S. plant. The U. S. loses its export advantage, and may become an importer.

The higher income of the U. S. consumer may lead the U. S. manufacturer to produce a more advanced version of the product. The scale-economies available to the U. S. manufacturer may make him competitive exporting this advanced version of the product, although the U. S. may be simultaneously importing less-advanced versions.

U. S. export performance in consumer durables seems to be affected by three variables: the appeal of the product to different income-groups, the availability of economies of scale, and the relative importance of transportation and duty costs.

The businessman can analyze the characteristics of his products in the light of these three variables to help him to identify opportunities for export and to forecast competition from imports.

ACKNOWLEDGEMENTS

I would like to thank the members of my thesis committee, Professors Raymond Vernon, Lawrence Fouraker, and Hugo Uyterhoeven, for their patient reading of drafts and helpful comments in the preparation of this thesis.

My deepest appreciation goes especially to Professor Vernon, who, along with Dean Horace Sturgis, formerly of Georgia Tech, was primarily responsible for my interest in continuing my studies for the doctorate. Professor Vernon's help and encouragement in the last three years have been many times that required of a teacher.

I would also like to thank my parents for their sacrifice and constant faith which have helped me through these years of studying and my wife, Margret, for her patience and help in leaving me free to work on this project. A thesis-writer is clearly not the best-possible husband for the first year of married life.

My thanks also go to the Ford Foundation, whose grant made possible the first stage of this thesis.

> Louis T. Wells, Jr.
> Boston
> June 1966

TABLE OF CONTENTS

TABLES

FIGURES

CHAPTER I

CONCEPTUALIZING FOREIGN TRADE FLOWS

International trade is a risky business. Patterns of trade are constantly shifting. New opportunities for exports are always appearing. New threats from imports seem to be forever appearing over the horizon. The businessman who thinks that he is simply a domestic operator and need not worry about foreign trade may suddenly find that his domestic market has turned to buying unexpected imports.

The importance of international trade is growing every year. The closer ties among countries, the increase in speed and the decrease in cost of transportation, the reduction of tariffs and other barriers to trade, and the ever increasing awareness of other markets and technologies resulting from the growth in communications have set in motion a growth in international trade which may be expected to continue for a long time into the future. The opportunities for profitable exports are increasing with the growth in trade. Alert American companies have seen the contribution of exports to their profits climb rapidly. However, the same factors which have created these opportunities for profit have also brought about increased vulnerability to the threat of competition from imports.

14

The businessman who survives and prospers in this
setting of constant change must be able to spot opportunities and
threats in advance so that he may react quickly. He cannot afford
to wait until someone else has demonstrated the existence of overseas markets, nor can he wait until imports are taking away a
substantial portion of his sales.

In order to be able to see in advance those shifts in trade
opportunities and threats which may affect him, the businessman
must have some framework for understanding the changing patterns
of international trade. He must be able to conceptualize the characteristics of products which determine whether they may be successfully marketed abroad, or whether they may be produced
abroad and marketed in the United States, threatening his domestic
market.

Part of the job of the economist has been to explain the
patterns of international trade. It is true that many of the theories
which have been advanced by the economists have been difficult to
use directly to help the businessman in solving his problems. However, many of these theories which were developed for broader
purposes may lend useful clues to the understanding of the process
of international trade.

Let us take a look at the theories which the economists have developed and try to extend them a bit to make them useful in explaining trade patterns in one particular field, consumer durables. Trade in consumer durables is in itself important, having accounted for 8.7% of world exports of manufactures in 1958, representing some $3.7 billion of trade.[1] However, the methods of conceptualizing trade flows in this one industry may be useful in approaching the problem of conceptualizing patterns in other related industries as well, especially those which are similarly not tied to locations in a particular country because of the availability of scarce raw materials and which are characterized by large scale-economies.

NEO-CLASSICAL THEORY

The theory of international trade has traditionally concentrated on the relative abundance of production factors in countries to explain patterns of trade. The best known statement of the tenets of traditional trade theory is the Heckscher-Ohlin theorem.

---

1. Maizels, A., R. Thomas and L. Boross, "Trends in World Trade in Durable Consumer Goods," National Institute Economic Review, No. 6, November 1959, p. 15.

This model states that a country will export products requiring
more of its abundant factors and import those items requiring
more of its scarce factors. [2]

The basic theory is intellectually pleasing. Its assumptions
are clearly stated and, at least for a two-country, two-product
model, the theory can be derived graphically or mathematically
from these assumptions. The theory, with its embelishments

---

2. Heckscher, Eli F., "The Effect of Foreign Trade on the
    Distribution of Income," American Economic Association,
    Readings in the Theory of International Trade, Blakiston
    Company, Philadelphia, 1950, pp. 272-300. Ohlin, B.
    Interregional and International Trade, Harvard Economic
    Studies, Vol. XXXIX, Cambridge, Mass., 1933. See
    Meier, Gerald M., International Trade & Development,
    Harper and Row, New York, 1963, Chapter 2, for a com-
    plete statement of the static general equilibrium model.
    Although Heckscher and Ohlin considered several cases
    under differing assumptions, the model described is the
    one commonly understood under the name Heckscher-
    Ohlin Theorem.

and expansions[3] offer an explanation for the volume, terms, and directions of international trade.

However, the theory was not developed primarily to explain existing patterns of trade. The classical and neo-classical economists were very much interested in developing models which could contribute to an understanding of the effects of trade on national and world welfare. Their models could be manipulated to yield clues to the effects of trade on returns to different factors of production in a country, to the results of devaluation, and to many other questions which interested the economic policy maker.

To build such models, the economists had to introduce very restrictive assumptions. These assumptions were certainly

_____

3. For summaries of classical and neo-classical theory, see:

Haberler, Gottfried, A Survey of International Trade Theory,
    International Finance Section, Princeton University, Re-
    vised Edition, Princeton, July 1961;
Chipman, John, "A Survey of the Theory of International Trade,"
    Parts 1 and 2, Econometrica, July and October 1965;
Bhagwati, J., "The Pure Theory of International Trade," The
    Economic Journal, March 1964, pp. 1-84.

not very accurate descriptions of reality: linear, homogeneous
production functions, perfect compstition, etc. However, they
were necessary to obtain sufficiently rigorous models which
could be manipulated to serve the purposes which interested the
macro-economists.

The trouble came when these models were used in an
attempt to explain observed trade patterns. Factors which had
been assumed away were often all important and completely ob-
scured the effects of the variables in the macro-models when
these models were applied to explain trade in individual products.
Changes did occur and equilibrium was never reached. competition
was imperfect and production functions were non-linear for many
products.

Leontief made the first large empirical test of the ability
of the neo-classical theory to explain broad patterns of international
trade. [4] By using his input-output tables for the United States
economy, he estimated the relative labor and capital utilization in
various industrial classifications. He then compared the labor/
capital ratios for United States exports with the ratios for imports,

4. Leontief, Wassily, "Domestic Production and Foreign Trade:
The American Capital Position Re-examined," Economia
Internazionale, February 1954, pp. 9-38.

assuming that the imports were produced with the same technology abroad as the United States industry employed. He discovered that the United States apparently exported labor-intensive goods and imported capital-intensive products. It had been assumed that the United States was capital-abundant, and, hence, according to the Heckscher-Ohlin model, should export capital-intensive goods. Leontief's finding was quickly named the "Leontief Paradox" and gave rise to a debate which has not yet subsided.

Leontief's findings were attacked on the basis of his methodology. Economists argued that his selection of 1947 as the year for his study biased his findings (Leontief re-did his calculations for 1951), that his assumptions about production functions were wrong, etc. However, Tatemoto and Ichimura[5] made a similar study for Japan and found that Japanese exports were capital-intensive while imports were labor-intensive. Japan certainly appeared to be a labor-abundant country. This study seemed to confirm the inability of the neo-classical theory to explain adequately the patterns of international trade.

5. Tatemoto, Masahiro and Shinichi Ichimura, "Factor Proportions and Foreign Trade: The Case of Japan," Review of Economics and Statistics, November 1959, pp. 442-46.

Leontief's results have caused trade theory to be developed along two different paths. Those economists following the first route have tried to keep a single, elegant model to explain trade patterns and their effects on the world and national economies. These economists have tried to vary the assumptions of the Heckscher-Ohlin theory slightly to make it describe reality better, or have tried to use other factors in addition to homogeneous labor and capital, or have tried to introduce limited dynamic elements into the static model. Those on the second path claimed that a single, elegant model could not yet explain the diverse patterns of trade in the world. Thus, the theory became fractionated, losing its universality and usefulness in explaining macro-phenomena. However, it gained, these economists hoped, in its ability to explain the observed patterns of international trade.

RECENT DEVELOPMENTS IN TRADE THEORY

Attempts to Retain the Heckscher-Ohlin Model

Leontief himself did not reject the Heckscher-Ohlin hypothesis. He concluded that the quality of the United States labor force was so high that the United States is really a labor-abundant country, not a capital-abundant one. Leontief's explanation has never found

much favor among economists. Kravis stated the counter-
argument well:

> In short, the United States is supplying
> the rest of the world with sufficient capital to
> produce goods equivalent in value to about half
> its imports. This is scarcely the position of a
> nation that has a capital shortage, particularly
> since the capital referred to, private direct in-
> vestment, represents, even in net terms, only
> about half the total United States long-term in-
> vestment abroad.[6]

Haberler suggests that Leontief should have taken into
account other factors, particularly natural resources and entre-
preneurship.[7] Bhagwati suggests that labor is not homogeneous
and that differences in skills may be accounted for by calculating
the capital embodied in education and training.[8]

6. Kravis, Irving B., "'Availability' and Other Influences on the
    Commodity Composition of Trade," Journal of Political
    Economy, Volume LXIV, No. 2, April 1956, p. 150.

7. See Corden, W. M., Recent Developments in the Theory of In-
    ternational Trade, International Finance Section, Princeton
    University, Princeton, 1965, p. 28.

8. For this and other adaptations of the Heckscher-Ohlin hypothesis,
    see Bhagwati, J., "Some Recent Trends in the Pure Theory
    of International Trade," Harrod, Roy (ed.), International
    Trade Theory in a Developing World, St. Martin's Press,
    Inc., New York, 1963, pp. 1-30. See also the discussion of
    the paper on pp. 393-405.

22

There are a number of other such suggestions for re-
tention of the Heckscher-Ohlin model. However, few have been
put to the test empirically. Donald Keesing[9] did perform a test
for research and development as a production factor. Although
Keesing does not explicitly say that he is retaining the Heckscher-
Ohlin model, he does state that his study is "highly compatible
with a view that the United States is specializing in skill-intensive
activities because of a comparative abundance of skilled relative
to unskilled labor." Keesing considers capital requirements and
natural resource requirements, but finds that the intensity of the
utilization of research and development is the best predictor of
United States export performance. He applies his tests only to
manufactures, implying a limitation of the universal applicability
of a simple version of the Heckscher-Ohlin model.

Other attempts to retain something similar to the Heckscher-
Ohlin view have been made by trying to adjust the model by changing
one of its assumptions. Minhas claimed that factor reversal occurs

9. Keesing, Donald, "Research, Development and American Trade
   Performance," to be published. See also: Keesing, "Labor
   Skills and Comparative Advantage," American Economic
   Review, May 1966, and Keesing, "Labor Skills and Inter-
   national Trade. Evaluating Many Trade Flows with a Single
   Measuring Device," Review of Economics and Statistics,
   August 1965.

in overseas production. [10] According to him, production that
is capital-intensive in the United States may be labor-intensive
abroad. Kindleberger agreed[11] and claimed that one should
compare the capital-labor ratios of the United States exports
with the capital-labor ratio of the exporting country for United
States imports, in other words change the Heckscher-Ohlin
assumption of identical production functions. However, Leontief
reworked Minhas' data and concluded that there was little evidence of factor cross-over. [12]

Any theory which retains the Heckscher-Ohlin emphasis
on relative abundance of production factors to explain trade seems
to be inadequate for the patterns of trade which are observed in

10. Minhas, Bagacha S., An International Comparison of Factor
     Costs and Factor Use, North-Holland Publishing Company,
     Amsterdam, 1963.

11. Kindleberger, Charles, Foreign Trade and the National
     Economy, Yale University Press, New Haven, 1962, pp. 75-77.
     See also, Ellsworth, P.T., "The Structure of American Foreign
     Trade: A New Word Examined," Review of Economics and
     Statistics, No. 36, 1954, pp. 279-285.

12. Leontief, E., "An International Comparison of Factor Costs
     and Factor Use," American Economic Review, Vol. 54,
     June 1964, pp. 335-345.

consumer durables. A particular country often is both an importer and an exporter of what appears to be the same product, at least when considered from the viewpoint of factor utilization. For example, the United States exports large refrigerators, but it imports small ones. It exports automobiles, but it also imports them. There appears to be no systematic difference in the factors utilized for the production of the exports and for the imports in many such cases.

Moreover, the neo-classical theory and most of the attempts to formulate adaptations of it were static. Equilibrium was assumed to be reached and no explanation was offered for transitional states. Keesing did try to explain some of the shifts in United States exports by examining the changes in research and development expenditures. He did not obtain very significant results in his statistical conclusions for changes in flows. The trade patterns which are observed do seem to be constantly shifting, apparently with little relation to changes in the relative abundance of production factors in various countries. For example, before World War II, the United States had a virtual monopoly in the exports of washing machines (98% of the market in 1937); by 1958, its share had fallen to 28%. Exports of refrigerators declined from the immediately prewar period to a

lower absolute volume in the 1960's despite the liberalization of
trade restrictions and the reduction in transportation costs. However, United States exports of movie cameras, dishwashers, and
room airconditioners have increased rapidly in recent years.

Fragmentation of Trade Theory

The route followed by the second group of economists seems
to offer more promise of help in the problems of the businessman.
This group moved away from the idea of a single model to explain
the observed patterns in the many types of goods in international
trade and simultaneously to perform the services of the Heckscher-
Ohlin model in explaining effects of changes in trade on the national
and world economies. [13] In sacrificing the comprehensiveness and
the intellectual appeal of the single, mathematical or geometrical
model, these economists did gain in accuracy in explaining observed patterns of trade.

---

13. It is interesting to note that Ohlin himself did not feel that the so-
called Heckscher-Ohlin model, even with adaptations, was
adequate to describe trade statistics. On p. 399 of Harrod,
op. cit., Ohlin claims that we need several models for
trade, using factor proportions, economies of large-scale
production, transport costs, and other elements.

It would be unfair to imply that all these economists did their work as a result of the Leontief Paradox. The direction had already been set by writers dealing with the "dollar shortage."[14]

These economists broke away from the restrictive, but very explicit, assumptions of the Heckscher-Ohlin model. They were willing to use different assumptions for different types of goods and to introduce dynamic elements. The majority were willing to keep something close to the Heckscher-Ohlin model for agricultural and natural-resource oriented products, but for manufactures, the approaches were numerous.

---

14. See, for example:

Balogh, T. Dollar Crisis, Oxford University Press, London, 1949;

Hansen, A. H., America's Role in the World Economy, W. W. Norton, New York, 1945;

Kindleberger, C. P., The Dollar Shortage, The Technology Press, Cambridge, 1950;

MacDougall, G. D. A., "British and American Exports: A Study Suggested by the Theory of Comparative Costs, Part 1," Economic Journal, December 1951, pp. 697-724;

Robertson, Sir Dennis, Britain in the World Economy, George Allen and Unwin, Ltd., London, 1954.

The writers provided a discussion of factors which appeared
to affect trade patterns. Many of these writers expressed their
analyses in non-mathematical form, sometimes with terms which
they had not yet been able to define clearly. Sometimes the hypothesis was not rigorous enough to allow for an empirical test.

Among these writers was Irving Kravis who provided an ex-
cellent preview of things to come. [15] Kravis argued that some goods
are simply not available in certain countries, i. e., the domestic
supply is inelastic. If unavailability is due to the lack of certain
natural resources, then the Heckscher-Ohlin type of explanation is
adequate. However, Kravis argues, there are other facets of availability which do not fit so well into the classical or neo-classical
framework. Kravis claimed, as had Balogh earlier, [16] that technological progress has a strong influence on trade. He claimed that
technological progress not only confers the advantages of a temporary cost reduction on the innovating country, but that it also gives
it the advantages of having the newest goods and the most recent
improvements in already existing ones. Kravis said that there is
a tendency for United States exports to shift continuously toward new
or improved products. He also considered product differentiation

---

15. Kravis, op. cit.

16. Balogh, op. cit.

28

and government policy to be important determinants of international trade. He turned toward the demand side and argued
that some consumers have preferences for products from particular countries -- Belgian lace, American cigarettes, etc.
This type of "national" product differentiation, as well as "firm"
product differentiation, gives some countries a sheltered position in foreign markets.

The technical gap concept, hinted at by Kravis, was
further developed by Posner[17] and then elaborated upon and empirically tested by Hufbauer[18] and by Douglass.[19] Hufbauer
proposes an imitation lag scale, by which countries can be placed
in a "pecking order." He argues and demonstrates that new
synthetics are usually introduced in the technically advanced
countries at the top of the "pecking order." These countries then
export to countries at the lower end. However, as time passes, the

17. Posner, M. V., "International Trade and Technical Change,"
    Oxford Economic Papers, October 1961, pp. 323-341.

18. Hufbauer, Gary C., Synthetic Materials and the Theory of
    International Trade, Gerald Duckworth and Company,
    London, 1965.

19. Douglass, Gorden K., Product Variation and International
    Trade in Motion Pictures, Ph.D. Thesis, Department of
    Economics, M.I.T., 1963.

technology becomes available to the lower order countries. Exports of these products from the advanced countries are displaced by production in the lower "pecking-order" countries, but they are replaced with newer, technically advanced products and the cycle continues with technology for each new product moving down the scale of countries.

Hufbauer was not very concerned with why a country took a particular position on the "pecking order." It was clear in his analysis that demand characteristics and market size had an important influence. Hufbauer admitted that he was unable to separate quantitatively the effects of the technological gap from scale economics. However, he did prove the usefulness of the technological lag concept in explaining trade patterns in at least one group of products, synthetic materials.

Douglass also used Kravis' "availability" concept and said that trade in the movie industry could be explained on the basis of product variation. He argued that there was an "imitation-lag", similar to Hufbauer's technological gap. When a country was once a leader, perhaps due to a larger supply of technological leadership, more research investment, or more favorable government attitudes and policies, that country would have a continuing ad-

30

vantage in related innovations, because one innovation in a sector creates a demand for improvements in related products. The country possessing the lead would, for a time, have an advantage in exporting products containing new innovations. Douglass claimed that the United States gained an early lead in the movie industry and was able to export successfully movies incorporating product innovations such as sound, color, and wide screen which were not yet available in the rest of the world. Douglass' explanation does not provide much help in predicting which countries will have a lead in innovation in other products, however.

An interesting attempt to retain the Heckscher-Ohlin emphasis on production factors but to introduce dynamic factors to explain the directions of trade is provided by Seev Hirsch.[20] Hirsch takes Kuznets' product cycle concept[21] and analyzes the changes in sales volume, production methods, factor inputs, prices, etc. which occur over the cycle. In the early phase of the product

20. Hirsch, Seev, Location of Industry and International Competitiveness, Doctoral Thesis, Harvard Business School, Boston, 1965.

21. Kuznets, S., Economic Change, W. W. Norton & Company, New York, 1953.

cycle, production runs are short and specification changes are frequent. The manufacturer is dependent on the availability of specialist suppliers and on the ability to communicate rapidly with them. Scientific and engineering inputs are critical, while costs may be less important due to lower price sensitivity for the individual firm at the new product stage. An abundance of skilled workers, special suppliers, and technical abilities would make a country competitive in this phase. The United States has an abundance of these factors, and hence, is competitive for new products, according to Hirsch:

> Using the language of the Heckscher-Ohlin theorem, it might be said that the U. S. is well endowed with production factors which are most needed in this phase. [22]

Later in the cycle, production runs become longer and specifications are standardized. Production processes and scale become fixed. The capital to labor ratio also becomes higher as special purpose machines are introduced. The price elasticity of demand for the output of the firm becomes very high. It is at this later stage that the United States loses its competitiveness.

---

22. Ibid., p. 48.

Other countries can easily obtain the technology and their labor skills are adequate. Their lower wage rates confer a cost advantage on them.

Hirsch's approach is useful in explaining many of the observed trade patterns. The hypothesis predicts that the United States is competitive in labor-intensive products, consistent with Leontief's findings. Hirsch applies his hypothesis to the electronics industry and finds it useful to explain trade in this industry. The hypothesis does not, however, explain the two-way trade in the same product with different qualities. Certainly the production processes for different size freezers or for transistor radios with different numbers of receiving bands are not very different. Moreover, many technically advanced, new products have been introduced in Europe and successfully exported. The product-cycle approach with emphasis almost entirely on supply factors does not adequately explain trade in these products.

Burenstam Linder[23] turned to the demand side for an explanation of trade flows in manufactures. He retained essentially the Heckscher-Ohlin model for primary products, but concluded that demand factors are critical to explain trade in manufactures.

---

23. Burenstam Linder, Staffan, An Essay on Trade and Transformation, Almqvist and Wiksells, Stockholm, 1961.

33

He argued that "representative" domestic demand is a necessary condition for an entrepreneur to manufacture a product. This manufacturer may attain a more "advantageous production function"[24] and is thus able to export to other countries with similar demands. A producer may be able to gain an "advantageous production function" through technological superiority, managerial skills, product differentiation, or economies of scale.

Burenstam Linder claims that demand characteristics are very closely related to per capita income. The same types of products have a similar demand in countries which have similar per capita income levels. A product which requires a high-income to have a large demand is likely to be introduced in a high-income country. One producer in a high-income country may gain an advantage and export to other countries. Since the largest demands are likely to be in similar markets, Burenstam Linder concludes that trade in manufactures will be most intense between countries of similar per capita income levels.

Burenstam Linder's hypothesis does help to explain trade patterns in consumer durables. Large refrigerators may have a more "representative demand" in the United States; small refrigerators, in Europe. Each country might have a more "ad-

---

24. Ibid., p. 102.

vantageous" production function in a different quality version of the product. Burenstam Linder says:

> The more representative the demand for a good is, the more likely it is that this good will be an actual export good. [25]

Although he does not conduct a very elaborate empirical test of his hypothesis, he does express his conclusions in a testable form and offers some figures which do tend to support his contention.

Raymond Vernon[26] takes an approach which combines the demand elements stressed by Burenstam Linder and the supply requirements discussed by Hirsch. Vernon argues that the United States market has a uniquely large demand for high-income and labor-saving products, due to its high per-capita income and its high cost of labor. A United States entrepreneur is more likely to be aware of the demand for products satisfying these needs and is, hence, more likely to develop such items.

---

25. Ibid., p. 103.

26. Vernon, Raymond, "International Investment and International Trade in the Product Cycle," to appear in Quarterly Journal of Economics.

This entrepreneur is also more likely to produce these products initially in the United States. The requirements of flexibility in product design, the low price elasticity of demand for the individual firm, and the need for close communication with the customers for new products argue for the location of the first production facility in the United States.

Some demand for the product may exist abroad almost immediately. The United States may then become an exporter. As production techniques settle down, some scale-economies may be reached and United States costs may be less than those of a potential small-scale producer abroad. However, as foreign markets grow, foreign production may be worthwhile. Vernon argues that transportation costs, factor costs, and the advantages of scale determine when foreign production will occur. At the point when foreign production starts, having lower-cost labor, the United States may lose its export advantage. So the United States appears to have an advantage in new, high-income or labor-saving products. As the product matures, the United States loses its advantage, but meanwhile, new products have been developed and the cycle begins again.

The following chapters will attempt to develop further a similar hypothesis, to test it against empirical data for consumer durables, and then to relate it to the findings of the other studies.

AN EXAMINATION OF ASSUMPTIONS

It might be useful, at this point, to list the assumptions
underlying the argument for the hypothesis proposed in the next
chapter and to compare them with the assumptions of the
Heckscher-Ohlin theory.

Production Functions

The Heckscher-Ohlin model is based on the assumption
of linear production functions. The hypothesis to be proposed
for consumer durables assumes that increasing returns-to-scale
are significant.

The importance of scale economies in modern manufacturing industry is well illustrated by the decline in the prices of the
Model-T Ford as production volume increased. Table I-1 shows
the price of the automobile from 1908 until 1916, as the production volume expanded from about 6,000 to almost 600,000 automobiles per year. It is, of course, not fair to attribute the total
price reduction to static scale-economies. For example, a
learning-curve concept would account for some of the increases
in efficiency over time. However, no doubt most of the reduction

Table I-1

Retail Price of Model-T Ford

Calendar Year	Retail Price (Touring Car)	Total Model-T Sales	Wholesale Price Index (1926=100)
1908	$ 850	5,986	62.9
1909	950	12,292	67.6
1910	780	19,293	70.4
1911	690	40,402	64.9
1912	600	78,611	69.1
1913	550	182,809	69.8
1914	490	260,720	68.1
1914	440	355,276	69.5
1916	360	577,036	35.5

Source: Rae, John B., The American Automobile: A Brief History, University of Chicago Press, Chicago, 1965, p. 61 and for the price index, U.S. Department of the Census, Historical Statistics of the United States, Colonial Times to 1957, Washington, D. C., 1960

was due to the increase in volume, allowing the introduction of assembly-line techniques. By early 1914, a full assembly-line was in operation.

Decreasing unit costs at larger scales result from a number of sources internal to the plant and firm.[27] For example,

1. The cost of some equipment and operations increases at a rate less than that of the increase in capacity. Examples are pipelines, bulk shipping, and design activities.

2. The required holdings of inventories, cash balances, etc. do not increase proportionally with volume.

3. Some of the equipment or operations for efficient production are indivisible. Most efficient production is obtained only at the lowest common multiple of the capacity of each price. Examples include stamping presses and assembly lines.

4. Larger-scale allows for the specialization of workers.

5. Management and staff functions may be integrated for several products.

6. Bulk buying and marketing may produce savings.

---

27. For a more extensive summary of economies of scale and external economies, see Chapters 6 and 7 of Balassa, Bela, The Theory of Economic Integration, R. D. Irwin, Inc., Homewood, 1961.

The significance of scale-economies is determined not only by the volume at which lowest-cost production occurs, but also by the rate of decline, or the steepness of the cost curve. The steepness determines, along with the price-elasticity of demand for the firm, the size of the disadvantage facing a plant operating below optimum capacity.

Estimates of optimal plant sizes[28] and the rate of decline of the cost curve with volumes below the optimal have been calculated by Bain and are well summarized in Belassa's work.[29] Table I-2 gives some of the results.

In addition to assuming that production functions are linear, the Heckscher-Ohlin model also assumes that they are homogeneous. Our hypothesis is based on the assumption that different pro-

---

28. The term "optimal plant size" is used to specify the size of a plant which is operating at a point at or very near the minimum unit cost obtainable. If unit costs continue to decline indefinitely, the "optimal plant size" is taken to mean the minimum size at which the penalties of not having a larger volume are not sufficient to drive the firm out of business in a situation where other producers do have larger volumes.

29. Belassa, op. cit., p. 139.

40

Table I-2

Optimal Plant Sizes for Several Products

	Approximate Optimal Plant Size		Increase of Unit Cost at 50% of Optimal Capacity	Increase of Unit Cost at 25% of Optimal Capacity
Automobiles	600,000	units		
Refrigerators	500,000	units		
Washing Mashines	500,000	units		
Rayon yarn	20,000-25,000	tons	8%	25%
Shoes	600,000-2,500,000	pairs	Insignificant	Moderate
Cement	400,000	tons	10%	30%
Crude Steel	1,000,000	tons	18%	33%
Cigarettes	20,000,000,000	units	1%	2%
Copper (Refined)	85,000	tons		

Source: Summarized from Belassa, *op. cit.*, Chapter 6

duction functions do exist, but that the disadvantages of small-volume production cannot be overcome by the substitution of cheap labor for capital in consumer durables, and, indeed, for most manufactured items which commonly enter world trade. We would expect to find similar production technologies in all countries where volumes are high. At much lower volumes, we would expect to find higher costs regardless of the kind of technology used. A. E. E. Robinson made a similar point:

> The number of bananas that could be produced by the labor required to build a locomotive would be widely different in Scotland and in the Canary Islands. But as regards a fairly considerable range of standard machine-produced products, it may be doubted whether the differences of relative efficiency are great. Goods are made in different countries with the help of almost identical machines. [30]

The automobile industry provides an illustration of both points; the existence of several technologies, but the utilization of essentially the same technology for the mass-produced automobiles which account for most of world trade in cars.

---

30. Robinson, A. E. A., The Structure of Competitive Industry, University of Chicago Press, Chicago, 1962, p. 144.

Methods of producing automobile bodies range from the hand-hammered bodies of the British Morgan (except for the fenders), through the fibreglass body of the Israeli Sabra and of many limited production British sports cars, to the mass-produced stamped parts used in General Motors, Ford, and Chrysler products all over the world, and by British Motors Corporation, Volkswagen, Mercedes Benz, etc. Volume of production, and not comparative labor costs, seems to be the determinant of which process is used. It is interesting to note that General Motors uses the more labor-intensive fibreglass process on the Corvette in the United States.

Similarly, different methods are available to manufacture mechanical and chassis components. The Morgan uses wood as body support material; the British Marcos uses marine plywood for its chassis. The Italian Lamborghini company builds its own engine parts on a very limited production basis.

All of these substitute technologies are apparently more expensive than mass-production, despite the fact that labor is cheaper in some of the countries. General Motors company officials have supposedly admitted that pressed-steel bodies would be cheaper than fibreglass at the present volume for the Corvette. The Morgan, which uses mechanical components from the Triumph

TR-4 (engine and several other parts) costs $3,175 (U. S. P. O. E.) versus $2,895 (U. S. P. O. E.) for the Triumph. The production volume of the Morgan is less than 500 per year. The Italian Lamborghini, with its own engine and body, costs $13,900 (U. S. P. O. E.), despite the lower Italian wages.

As soon as volume is sufficient, the automobile producers all appear to use the same technology, no matter what the relative labor costs are. Dean Bladen made the observation for the automobile industry after trips to several countries:

> As far as the mass producers are concerned,
> the technology is almost identical. I was
> really seeing the same thing each time. [31]

The special purpose, limited-production automobiles account for only a small percentage of the volume of automobile trade. The majority of trade is in Ford, General Motors, Chrysler, Volkswagen, Fiat, etc. products which are all built by essentially the same methods.

---

31. Bladen, Vincent, "Canada and the Motorcar: The Royal Commissioner Adds a Human Postscript," Varsity Graduate, Christmas, 1961, (University of Toronto), p. 58.

44

Studies which have looked at costs of manufactures produced in small volume in low-wage countries tend to confirm
the dominance of this scale-factor. Barlow concludes in his
Mexican study:

> The lower cost of foreign labor will not
> be sufficient to lower manufacturing costs below
> the United States level in industries where a
> heavy investment in machinery and tools is re-
> quired, unless the market is large enough to ab-
> sorb a volume permitting economic production
> runs. [32]

Table I-3 shows comparative prices of refrigerators and freezers
in Mexico and in the United States. Table I-4 gives production
figures for the two countries. Differences in material costs certainly could not account for the large differences in prices. No
doubt, most of the difference is explained by the difference in volume.

Empirical studies on the substitution of labor for capital in
low-wage countries have been sorely lacking. One such study is
presently being undertaken. [33] Preliminary results seem to show

---

32. Barlow, E. R., Management of Foreign Manufacturing Sub-
    sidiaries, Division of Research, Harvard Business School,
    Boston, 1953.

33. By Wayne Yeoman, as a doctoral thesis at the Harvard
    Business School.

Table I-3

Prices of Refrigerators and Freezers, United States and Mexico

Refrigerator Prices

Capacity in cu. ft.	U. S. Price (1965)	Mexican Price (1959)
6. 0 and under	$	$ 240 - 256
6. 2	219	
8. 6		304 - 400
9. 0		311 - 400
10. 8	170	
12. 0		544 - 640
12. 3	200	
14. 0		640 - 704
14. 2	340	

Freezer Prices

4. 0		344
6. 4	160	
7. 0		432
10. 0	180	536

Source: Mexican retail prices from U. S. Department of Commerce,
    Major Household Appliances: Production, Consumption, Trade,
U. S. Government Printing Office, Washington, 1960.

U. S. prices from Sears, Roebuck and Co., Catalog,
Fall and Winter, 1965.

Table I-4

Production of Refrigerators and Freezers in Mexico and United States

	U. S. Production (1963)	Mexican Production (1959)
Refrigerators	4,217,209 units	44,000 units
Freezers	1,037,644	1,850[*]

[*] 1958

Source: For United States, 1963 Census of Manufactures;
For Mexico, United States Department of Commerce,
Major Household Appliances, p. 33.

47

that, for American subsidiaries operating abroad, the prospective
savings due to the use of more cheap labor do not seem to warrant
major changes in the technology in low-wage countries for many
industries. The degree of change seems to be a function of the
price-elasticity for the firm, the capital-intensity of the industry,
and whether the industry is "heavy" or "light." The total degree
of substitution does not seem to be extremely large in any case.
The data appear to show that substitution of labor is less as the
scale becomes larger.

No doubt, agricultural production and home construction
are performed very differently in low-wage countries than in high-
wage ones. However, for most manufactured goods which enter
world trade, the evidence seems to point to the conclusion that,
despite the availability of alternative technologies, large-scale
production tends to be conducted in all countries by essentially
the same technology and that small-scale production, even with
lower wage-rates, is seldom cheaper than mass-production techniques used in a country with higher wage-rates. In other words,
unless labor is practically a free good, the savings obtained by
substituting cheap labor for capital at low volumes are seldom
greater than the savings gained from increasing volume to a point
where a more efficient technology may be used.

Perfect Competition

The Heckscher-Ohlin model assumes that the prices of
production factors are equal to their marginal products and that
the prices of products equal their marginal costs. Perfect
knowledge of the market is assumed. In contrast, our model
assumes that the entrepreneur does not have perfect knowledge
of all markets. No restriction is placed on the price of factors.
Prices of products in the short run are not necessarily equal to
their marginal costs in the situation of imperfect competition.

Barriers to Trade

In contrast to the Heckscher-Ohlin assumption that transportation and tariff costs are zero, the model to be developed
assumes that they are not negligible. One estimate of transportation costs is given in Table I-5 which shows transportation
costs to supply British markets with products from United States
plants. Transportation appears to amount to at least 10% of production costs in many cases. For industrial areas, tariffs of 10%
to 30% are very common. Table III-26 gives the tariffs for selected consumer durables for several countries.

Table I-5

Transportation Costs to Supply British Markets from United States Plants

Cost of Transportation	Percentage of Cases
less than 10% of production costs	40%
10-20%	25
20-30	22
Over 30	13

NOTE: There is probably an upward bias in the data due to the selection of products which were already being produced by subsidiaries of United States firms in Britain.

Source: Dunning, John H., American Investment in British Manufacturing Industry, George Allen and Unwin, Ltd., London, 1958, p. 233.

Factor Mobility

The Heckscher-Ohlin model assumes that factors are
completely mobile within regions, but that they may not move
across boundaries. We assume that labor is not mobile across
boundaries, but that capital is, although not necessarily without
friction. The growth of the multinational corporations with their
access to various capital markets has tended to increase the mo-
bility of capital, especially among the industrial countries. [34]
It is no longer adequate to assume very different costs of capital
for all investors in different countries.

Static Equilibrium

The Heckscher-Ohlin theorem assumes full-employment,
static equilibrium. Our model assumes that static equilibrium is
not reached and assumes that changes in technology and growth in
incomes occur.

The Model and Empirical Test

The next chapter develops an explanation of trade in certain
manufactures based on these assumptions. The results of an empirical test of the explanation are then presented in Chapter III.

---

34. See Vernon, op. cit.

The final chapter attempts to relate the findings to the other hypotheses and studies discussed in this chapter and to indicate the possibilities of using such models for business planning.

CHAPTER II

AN HYPOTHESIS TO DESCRIBE TRADE PATTERNS IN CONSUMER DURABLES

This chapter will propose an hypothesis to explain trade patterns in consumer durables based on the assumptions presented in Chapter I. The approach will sacrifice the comprehensiveness of a macro-model, but should gain in accuracy in describing patterns for the particular group of products. The hypothesis will not be able to explain shifts in the performance of this broad group of products relative to other categories, nor will it help to explain the effects of some national economic policies on trade patterns. These tasks will be left to the macro-economist. He must, though, in his efforts to present a general model, ignore many of the variables which affect the individual products which are of concern to the businessman. In fact, these variables may be of such importance on the micro-level as to obscure completely the effects of the variables which interest the macro-economist.

The results of an empirical test of the hypothesis will be presented in Chapter III. Although the test was conducted only for United States exports of consumer durables, much of the argument may be applicable to a wider range of products.

INTRODUCTION OF A NEW PRODUCT

Let us start the analysis by looking at the process by which a new product is created and brought to the market to see if we can determine where a new product is likely to be introduced. The process can be somewhat arbitrarily divided into three distinct stages, although the division may not be clear for every product. The first stage is the generation of some basic scientific knowledge; the second stage is the use of that scientific knowledge to create a product which satisfies some need; and the third stage is the commercial manufacture of the product.

The first stage is usually clearly distinguishable from the others. Most of our household appliances are based on simple Newtonian physics plus a knowledge of electricity from Faraday. Transistors are based on the theories of solid-state physics. In many cases, a number of years elapses from the time when the basic scientific knowledge is developed until a particular product is created based on this knowledge. For example, the principles upon which photography is based were developed by Leonardo da Vinci some 500 years ago, but the first workable process was created in 1839. Faraday developed the principles for the electric motor in the 1830's, but it was not used industrially until the

1870's. Radio broadcasting was based on the work of Maxwell
and Hertz, between 1873 and 1899, but a working radio was not
created until 1904, and commercial radio did not exist until the
1920's. There is some evidence, though, that the time gap
between the basic knowledge and the practical application is decreasing.

The second and third stages, the creation of a product
and the commercial manufacture, may not be as clearly separable.
The developer of the first product must usually make a pilot model.
Product development and improvement generally continue while
more models are made. Somewhere along the process, commercial sales begin, but usually product changes continue as more
knowledge of market requirements is available. Somewhere in
these two stages, the entrepreneur enters the picture. Product
development and certainly production can be expensive. Someone
must provide the capital for these stages. Later sections will discuss these phases further. Let us now return to the first stage,
the creation of the necessary basic scientific knowledge, and look
at it in more detail.

---

1. These examples are from Johnson, Earl O., "The Aerospace
   Industry," pp. 60-81 of Ginzberg, Eli, Technology and
   Social Change, Columbia University Press, New York,
   1964.

Basic Scientific Knowledge

The findings of pure science and basic engineering are today generally quickly known throughout the industrialized world. The economist has usually assumed that basic scientific knowledge was a free good. [2] Much of the basic scientific knowledge is generated by universities and private foundations. (See Table II-1) These organizations depend for their success on the reputation which they gain by connecting their names with the publishing of their findings, rather than on a competitive advantage obtained by keeping the knowledge a secret. Articles describing findings appear quickly in the some 50,000 technical journals which contain around 1,200,000 articles per year. The chemical abstracts alone contain some 13,000 pages per year. [3] These journals enjoy a wide circulation throughout the developed world, (See Table II-2). The other large producer of basic scientific knowledge is the government, primarily through its military and space programs. Daniel Bell thinks that the scientific knowledge generated in this sector is not very useful in the civilian sector.

---

2. See for example, Grubel, Herbert G., and A. D. Scott, "International Flows of Human Capital," American Economic Review, May 1966.

3. Bell, Daniel, "The Post-Industrial Society," in Ginzberg, Eli, op. cit., p. 45.

57

Table II-1

Basic Research in the Life and Physical Sciences, 1953-1954

Major Sector Performing	Percent of Total Basic Research Expenditures
Federal Government Agencies	11%
Industry-Oriented Organizations[*]	39
Colleges and Universities	47
Other Institutions	3

[*] P. 28 of the source indicates "A large part - perhaps the major part - of what industry regards as basic research would be considered to be applied research and development in universities."

Source: National Science Foundation, Basic Research, A National Resource, United States Government Printing Office, 1957, p. 30.

Table II-2

Foreign Circulation of Selected U. S. Scientific Journals

Publication	U.S. Circulation	Foreign Circulation
American Chemical Society Journals		
Biochemistry	4,556	1,290
Chemical Reviews	5,906	2,317
Inorganic Chemistry	4,567	1,198
Analytical Chemistry	29,731	8,034
Physics Today	45,511	3,440
Science	111,719	6,461

Source: Business Publications: Rates and Data, Standard Rate and Data Service, Inc., Skokie, Ill., Feb. 24, 1966.

59

Most of the growth of science today, which is in
the military sector, is not easily adapted to the
civilian sector. ... There is little spillover from
industries involved in space development into the
civilian sector of the economy. What the government spends on military or space devices rarely
makes a direct or even slow indirect contribution
to the civilian sector. [4]

Even if the conclusion that most government-generated
findings will never make a contribution to the civilian sector seems
like a dangerous forecast, it does appear reasonable to conclude
that the time lag from theory to application will be long enough
such that the basic scientific knowledge will be available to all industrial countries by the time that civilian products are generated.

It appears, then, that the possession of some basic scientific knowledge not available to the rest of the industrialized world
is seldom significant in providing a competitive advantage to a
particular country in the world market.

Product or Process Development

The second and third stages of product creation offer more
hints as to the directions of trade flows. It is useful, for clarifi-
cation, to separate the second stage into two types, depending on

4. Bell, Daniel, op. cit., p. 53.

the kind of product under discussion. One type of development
is centered on the product itself, while another type is centered
on the process of making the product. Most of the familiar consumer durables fall into the first group. Basic physics proposed
the principles upon which the electric washing machine was based.
The problem for the designer was to put the principles together
and to create a workable machine. The metal working techniques
were well known for producing the final product. Penicillin is an
illustration of the other category. The basic composition of
penicillin was known some time before the introduction of the
product on the market. The problem for the designer was to find
a feasible commercial process to manufacture this product which
was clearly described by the biochemist. The early work of
Fleming, Raistrick, Thom, and others was undertaken primarily
as part of a search for an understanding of the phenomena of mold.
Their work was picked up by groups in the United States and in the
United Kingdom which were interested in practical applications.
The development of a commercial process to produce penicillin
waited for the terrific demands created by World War II. [5] Many

5. For a more detailed history of the development of penicillin,
    see the statement of David Novick before the Antitrust and
    Monopoly Subcommittee of the Senate Judiciary Committee,
    reproduced in Bright, James R., Research, Development
    and Technological Innovation, Richard D. Irwin, Homewood,
    1964, pp. 21, 27.

of the products of the chemical industry fit into this second category, while most of the products of the metal-working industries fall into the first.

What can be said about this process or product development stage? The old adage, "necessity is the mother of invention," may have more truth than economists have generally credited it with. Empirical knowledge in the area of invention has been sorely lacking. However, a recent study has gone a long way toward showing that invention is not self-generating, but that it is inspired by specific demand. [6]

6. Schmookler, Jacob, Invention and Economic Growth, Harvard University Press, Cambridge, Mass., 1966, (June). See also: Bright, James R., op. cit., p. 61. "Unlike fundamental scientific research, design is motivated by need rather than by curiosity," Burenstam Linder, Staffan, op. cit., pp. 88-89; Griliches, Levi, and Jacob Schmookler, "Inventing and Maximizing," American Economic Review, Vol. LIII, No. 4, September 1963, pp. 725-729; Schmookler, Jacob, "Economic Sources of Inventive Activity," Journal of Economic History, Vol. XXII, March 1962, pp. 1-20; and for a summary of the earlier literature, see Richard R. Nelson's "Introduction" to Universities - National Bureau Committee for Economic Research, The Rate and Directions of Inventive Activity: Economic and Social Factors, Princeton University Press, Princeton, 1962.

It appears that in the majority of cases the process or product development will be done by someone who is familiar with a potential demand for the product. It seems unlikely, for example, that a German who had never travelled abroad would design an electric home ice-crusher. Germans do not commonly use crushed-ice in their drinks; hence he is unlikely to be aware of the need for such a device. However, an American is certainly aware of a potential market and is much more likely to invent such an item.

Commercial Production

Somewhere in the stage of product or process development the entrepreneur will appear. With some types of products, a single designer or inventor can develop alone a product or process to a stage where it is marketable. With other types of products, the expenses are large and risk capital is required to continue the development almost from the beginning. For commercial production, in any case, financing from the entrepreneur is necessary. This section will discuss who this entrepreneur is likely to be and where he is likely to start production.

The entrepreneur providing the capital is doing so in the hope of making a profit. He must make a calculation of the probability of commercial success for the product and weigh the prospective

gains against his possible losses. The first requirement is
some estimate of the size of the market for the product. If
the awareness of potential demand was a likely prerequisite for
the inventor, it is an absolute necessity for the entrepreneur.
If by some quirk the German did invent an home electric ice-
crusher, it would be unlikely that he could interest a German
entrepreneur in investing in production for the German market.

Why, though, might the German entrepreneur not produce for the United States market? The classical economists assume that market knowledge is universally available as a free
good. However, many modern writers are moving away from
this assumption. Typical of this trend is the following from
Burenstam Linder:

> Firstly, the decision to take up production of
> any particular good is likely to be generated
> by clearly discernible economic needs. In a
> world of imperfect knowledge, entrepreneurs
> will react to profit opportunities of which they
> are aware. These would tend to arise from
> domestic needs. Perhaps a need that an entre-
> preneur has himself experienced has provided
> the idea on which his entrepreneurship is based. [7]

7. Burenstam Linder, Staffan, op. cit., p. 88.

Why does the entrepreneur not search out market
information from other countries? Two explanations exist
for his behavior. The first is based on the behavioral model
of Herbert Simon, which he called the "Administrative Man"
and on the similar concept of C. P. Kindleberger which he
entitles "economic horizons." The second explanation is
based on the empirical study of Ward Edwards.

The first concept is expressed as follows by Kindleberger:

> A man may be perfectly rational, but only
> within a limited horizon....As a producer,
> he will sell his goods typically in a given
> ambit. Over his horizon there may lie bril-
> liant opportunities to improve his welfare as
> a consumer or his income as a producer, but
> unless he is made aware of them, they will
> avail him nothing. [8]

---

8. Kindleberger, Charles P., Foreign Trade and the National
    Economy, p. 16. See also Simon, H. A., "Theories in
    Decision Making in Economics and Behavioral Science,"
    American Economic Review, Vol. XLIX, June 1959, pp.
    253-284; and March, James G. and H. A. Simon, Or-
    ganizations, John Wiley and Sons, New York, 1958; and
    Simon, H. A., Administrative Behavior, MacMillan,
    New York, 1958. An interesting statement of a similar
    idea is given in Lee, James A., "Cultural Analysis in
    Overseas Operations," in Harvard Business Review,
    March-April 1966, pp. 106-114. Lee uses the term "self
    reference criterion" to describe a similar phenomenon.

65

The horizons of an entrepreneur are determined partly by
geographical distance. He is less familiar with far away
places and the cost of obtaining more information is high.
Cultural differences also play a significant role. Kindleberger notes the large amount of trade between the United
Kingdom and New Zealand. No doubt, the common cultural
heritage and resultant close communication of the two societies
makes the businessman in each country more aware of the opportunities in the other. The horizons of an entrepreneur seem
to be, as Burenstam Linder concluded, limited to an area which
approximates national borders, although a more accurate in-
terpretation would probably define the market area somewhat
differently. [9]

The German entrepreneur considering the production of a
home electric ice-crusher may, however, have heard that Americans put crushed ice in their drinks. He might consider investing

---

9. Besides the example of the British Commonwealth where the
United Kingdom businessman may be so familiar with other
similar markets in the group, Belgiums seem to be an important case. It appears that the horizons of certain
Belgium businessmen now include at least the BENELUX
area.

some money to obtain more market knowledge about the United
States. The empirical evidence of Ward Edwards suggests a
reason why he is unlikely to do this, or if he should do it, why
he is unlikely to act on the result. Edwards found that indi-
viduals tend to overestimate the probability of unlikely events,
and to underestimate the information content of small samples. [10]
The German entrepreneur is likely not to invest in the market
information as he will underestimate its value. Moreover, if he
does make the investment, he is still likely to make a pessi-
mistic forecast of his chances of success in the United States.

These two arguments would lead to the conclusion that
an entrepreneur is most likely to invest in production for his
home market. [11]

---

10. Edwards, Ward, in Journal of Experimental Psychology,
     Vol. 52, 1956, pp. 177-187.

11. The widely quoted counter-example to this contention is
     the case of Japan. However, an empirical study of the
     Japanese economy revealed that "Japan tended to ex-
     port manufactures of the same general type as those
     used extensively by her own people." See Lockwood,
     W. W., The Economic Development of Japan, Prince-
     ton University Press, Princeton, 1954, p. 373.

American Uniqueness

The conclusion that an entrepreneur is most likely to invest in production for his home market provides a way to look at what types of products are likely to be appealing to an American entrepreneur, but not to a foreigner. It is only necessary to look at what characteristics of the American market are unique.

The United States has the largest high-income market in the world. [12] Hence, the United States entrepreneur is likely to be the first to invest in products with an appeal primarily to high-income customers. The electric can opener and the electric knife sharpener were first introduced in America, for example. Both of these products appealed primarily to the high-income segment of the market. However, stainless steel razor blades were first introduced overseas. This product, however, appeals to a much wider market (see Table II-3).

------

12. The per capita GNP of the United States for 1958 was $2,343. The next highest were Canada, with $1,667; New Zealand, with $1,249; and Switzerland with $1,229. Only seven other countries had a figure over $1,000. The GNP of the U.S. was $387,200 million, while the U.K., with $51,100 was the second highest. Only two countries in the Western World had a total GNP over 1/10 of the United States'. See Burenstam Linder, op. cit., Matrix 1, following p. 116.

Table II-3

Income-Groups Owning Electric Knife Sharpeners, Electric Can Openers,
or Purchasing Stainless Steel Razor Blades

For households where the head was college educated, white collar, the following tables gives
the percentage owning the appliances:

Income	Households as % of Sample	Percentage of Households Owning Elec. Knife Sharpener	Percentage of Households Owning Elec. Can Opener	Percentage of Men Who Bought Stainless Steel Razor Blades in the Past Month
$10,000 or more	8.5%	21.5%	18.8%	12.0%
Under $10,000	8.4	11.6	10.0	11.0

The pattern is even stronger for the non-college educated.

Source: Time Marketing Services, Selective Mass Markets for Products and Services, 1964 data, pp. 18-19.

United States as Location of Production

Although an American entrepreneur is likely to be the
first to invest in a new product appealing primarily to a high-
income market, no argument has been given why he should
locate his production facilities in the United States. It seems
that the entrepreneur considering the production of an electric
knife sharpener or electric can opener might well have started
production in Germany, where wage rates are lower, using
capital obtained in the United States. [13] He might well calculate
that the additional costs of transportation and duty would not be
great enough to offset the savings in labor costs. He might also
find that his materials cost, primarily steel, would be as cheap,
if not cheaper than in the United States. Certainly, for most

---

13. According to the responses of 147 U. S. companies operating
abroad, labor, selling and distribution costs are lower
abroad, material costs are higher, and there is no significant difference in plant overhead and general administrative
costs. See Gates, Theodore, and Fabian Linden, Costs and
Competition: American Experience Abroad, National Industrial Conference Board, 1961.

Kreinan found that the higher cost of United States labor was
not offset by a sufficiently higher rate of productivity. See
Kreinan, Mordecai, "The Leontief Scarce-Factor Paradox,"
American Economic Review, March 1965, pp. 131-139.

consumer durables, the materials are readily available in all the industrialized countries. Their availability is certainly not an adequate explanation of production location. Why, then, does he not produce in Germany? Actually, there are several reasons why the American entrepreneur will probably choose to locate his plant in the United States.

The same behavioral models apply to the entrepreneur when he is deciding where he should locate his plant as when he is viewing potential markets. His horizons or list of alternatives may simply not include overseas locations. Moreover, if he has heard that labor is cheap overseas, he still may overestimate the problems which he might encounter and underestimate the advantages which might accrue to him.

However, there are other, more "rational" reasons why the entrepreneur might locate his production in the United States. One of these is the need for close contact with the customer to meet his demands as to product design. A new product is constantly changing as more information about customer requirements reaches the producer. The producer who is located far from his market is at a disadvantage in that communication is less perfect and takes more time. [14] Having the marketing and

---

14. See Hirsch, *op. cit.*, Chapters 3 and 5.

production departments in close proximity gives more assurance that rapid changes may be made to meet consumer requirements. Moreover, service requirements may be large and varied. As product design changes, the service people must be in contact with the production personnel to be aware of the changes and of their effects on their duties. Moreover, their service problems must be communicated to the design personnel so that changes may be instituted to eliminate problems. All of these communications will be more expensive and difficult as the production facilities are located farther from the primary market.

Moreover, external economies often play a significant role in new products. [15] As design changes occur, changes in production must be made. Many elements are subcontracted to specialists due to the short runs of a particular design. Materials requirements may change rapidly. Hence, the producer of the new product will benefit if he can be in close contact with special suppliers. There will be a relative abundance of such suppliers located in the United States because of the large number of new products introduced here for the other reasons.

---

15. See, for example, Max Hall (ed.), Made in New York, Harvard University Press, Cambridge, 1959, especially pp. 12-14.

Moreover, the new manufacturer is likely to be less concerned about cost at this stage. His customers may want the
product at any price if it meets their needs. Products are highly
differentiated and difficult for the customer to compare as to
price. W. E. G. Salter has observed this price-inelasticity of
new products:

> Even though methods and techniques may be very
> crude, it is often economic to begin production
> almost immediately, because a high price may be
> charged. [16]

If the new product is an industrial one which replaces
an old product by performing the same function better, the industrial customer will base his willingness to purchase on the
savings which will accrue to him. He will be willing to pay any
price as long as the savings are larger. If the product is a consumer product, there will be some customers who will pay a
relatively high price in order to be the first in their group to
own one. [17]

---

16. Salter, W. E. G., Productivity and Technical Change,
    Cambridge University Press, 1960, p. 133.

17. "Demand is likely to be relatively inelastic during a pro-
    duct's early stages, especially in consumer goods....
    The initial high price captures that segment which is
    relatively insensitive to price," Matthews, John B., Jr.,
    R. Buzzell, T. Levitt, and R. Frank, Marketing: An
    Introductory Analysis, McGraw-Hill Book Company, New
    York, 1964, pp. 243-244.

A number of reasons exist why the production of a new
product appealing to a high-income market will first occur in
the United States. However, these have not explained why the
United States may become an exporter of some of these products.

TRADE IN THE NEW PRODUCT

The United States' Advantage in Exports

Although foreign per capita incomes are lower than
United States incomes, foreign demand is not zero for a product
which appeals to a high-income population. The distribution of
incomes in other countries would indicate that there may be at
least some demand for the product abroad. Foreigners will
hear of the new product and will demand it either of importers
or directly of the United States manufacturer. Eurenstam Linder
cites the extreme example of what he calls "unrepresentative
demand" with the case of Cadillacs for Saudi Arabia. Another
example is the use of American electric dishwashers (until
recently) in the homes of wealthy Swiss families. Soon after the
introduction of the new product some exports from the United
States are likely to occur. As the United States market becomes

more saturated, the American producer may find himself with
excess capacity. He may put more effort into export markets
to utilize this capacity.

Let us look at what determines the quantity of these exports and how long they can be expected to continue.

Above a certain level of demand, a foreigner will probably
begin production for his own market. There are several factors
that will determine when this will occur. First, the market size
is determined by the income levels represented[18] and by the
appeal of the product to these income levels. The American producer will have gained some scale economies (an idea of the size
of U. S. companies compared to those of other countries can be
obtained from Table II-4), and thus can produce more cheaply
than a potential foreign producer if the market size is too small

18. "In general it appears that income is the main determinant of
ownership, but that there are a large number of other
factors." Maizels, A., op. cit., p. 122.

"Until a saturation level is reached, ownership is directly related
to household income," according to Sultan, Ralph G. M.,
An Econometric Analysis of the Demand for Nine Consumer Durables, Ph. D. thesis, Department of Economics,
Harvard University, 1964, p. 459.

Table II-4

Industrial Corporations Grouped According to Their
1964 Sales in $ Million

	Over 2000	1000-2000	500-1000	250-500	Together
U.S.	20	35	67	125	247
Total non U.S.	5	16	66	80	167
Canada			5	5	10
EEC	1	11	29	23	64
Belgium			2	1	3
France		1	11	9	21
Germany		8	10	10	28
Italy		1	5	2	8
Netherlands	1	1	1	1	4
EFTA	4	3	19	33	59
UK	4	2	15	28	49
Sweden			2	3	5
Switzerland		1	2	2	5
Japan		2	10	15	27
Other			3	4	7
	25	51	135	205	414

Source: Calculated by Balassa from Fortune, July and August, 1965.

abroad.[19] The foreigner, though, has the protection of tariff
and transportation costs (an idea of the magnitude of the protection offered by transportation costs can be gleaned from
Table II-5), and usually lower factor costs. He will probably
start production when his costs at the level of demand which
he expects to capture are less than those of the foreigner's
costs (perhaps incremental costs) plus transportation and duty.
Stephen Hymer has noted, for example, that local tire production

---

19. The importance of market size for productivity is discussed
in Paige, D. and G. Bombach, A Comparison of National
Output and Productivity in the United Kingdom and the United
States, O.E.C.D., Paris, 1959;

in Young, J. H., "Comparative Economic Development:
Canada and the United States," American Economic Review,
May, 1955, pp. 80-93;

and in Chenery, H. B., "Patterns of Industrial Growth,"
American Economic Review, September 1960, pp. 624-654.

Of course, there may be some small manufactures who
start early overseas. They may be able to sell at prices
higher than those of United States imports by providing
features especially suited to the market. Note, for example,
the existence of many small automobile producers in Europe
before the introduction of mass-production there. These producers were generally supplying a very high-income segment
of the European market with a type of automobile not yet mass-
produced in the United States (see the last section of this
chapter). It was not until after the First World War that the
assembly-line appeared in Europe, according to Rae, op. cit.,
p. 67.

Table II-5

Average Unit Cost of Washing Machines and Refrigerators
Produced in Japan

Year	Quantity Produced	Average unit value of Washing Machines Produced	Quantity Produced	Average unit value of Refrigerators Produced*
1951	3,328	n. a.	1,998	401
1952	15,117	n. a.	3,587	418
1953	104,679	n. a.	7,470	220
1954	265,552	$ 55	16,990	258
1955	461,267	51	30,571	207
1956	754,458	47	81,207	171
1957	854,564	48	231,241	142
1958	988,309	47	414,772	127
1959 (prelim.)	1,189,034	46	549,433	122

* Up until 1957, a part of the decline of the average value of a refrigerator may be attributed to a decline in size as a mass market developed. Perhaps about a 5% annual decline may be attributed to the reduced costs, though. See "Tokai Electric Company," ICH 8M31, case written by Mr. Shoto Fujieda of the Keio Business School.

There is no indication of a similar decline in the quality of the washing machines.

Source: Calculated by the author from Table 84 of U. S. Department of Commerce, Business & Defense Services Administration, Major Household Appliances: Production, Consumption, Trade, U. S. Government Printing Office, Washington, 1960, p. 138.

occurs as soon as the market size approaches 50, 000 tires a
year. [20] The United States should have a greater export advantage in items which have more protection from returns-to-
scale, which appeal to a higher-income consumer, and which
have lower transportation costs and foreign duties, all other
things being equal in each case. [21]

The share of the market which the foreigner can expect
to obtain is reduced if the product is highly differentiated or if
the importer has some kind of control over channels of distribution. In this case, the foreigner can gain little by under-
cutting the prices of the imports. However, as the product
moves to the "maturity stage" in its life cycle, product differentiation becomes more difficult and price becomes more
important as a determinant of market share. [22] In fact, the

20. Hymer, Stephen, The Theory of Direct Investment, (doctoral
    dissertation, M.I.T., 1960), p. 122.

21. The terms "return to scale" and higher-income appeal" have
    been used without very precise definitions in this section.
    The next chapter defines them more exactly.

22. See Levitt, Theodore, "Exploit the Product Life Cycle,"
    Harvard Business Review, November-December 1965,
    p. 83.

foreign producer may include some segments of foreign markets
in his calculation of what he can sell. The United States producer
has demonstrated the size of some markets through exports. The
foreigner is especially likely to include foreign markets in his
calculations if he or his competitors has been exporting related
products to these markets, and thus has channels of distribution
already established.

Deterioration of the American Export Position

The last section argued that foreign production would be
likely to occur when the foreign market reached a certain size.
With the introduction of overseas production, the United States
export performance deteriorates from what it would otherwise
have been, by the loss of at least a part of the market where the
production was introduced.

In many cases, the product for which manufacture is in-
itiated abroad is a lower quality version of the product which is
being produced in the United States. Lower quality, in this sense,
means a product which performs the same function, but is smaller,
has less automatic features, or has other cost reducing features.
A non-automatic washing machine would, in this sense, be lower
quality than an automatic machine. [23] The refrigerators produced

---

23. See also Burenstam Linder, op. cit., p. 95.

in Europe are generally smaller than the American ones, for example. Similarly, the performance specifications of the Volkswagen are very close to those of the American Model A Ford of 35 years ago. Because incomes are lower abroad, such products are often more suited to the demand of the local market.

As the foreigner attains larger-scale production, using a technology very similar to the United States manufacturer (See Chapter I), his costs decline (See Table II-5 for an example) such that his production costs plus transportation and duties are lower than the United States manufacturer's cost plus transportation and duties in third markets. The United States may then begin to lose third markets. If an "inferior" version of the product is being produced overseas, this loss may occur sooner. A good example is provided by the decline of the United States exports of automobiles to the less-developed countries having no local production, where Volkswagen, Peugeot, etc. have been successful and by the decline of the United States appliance market in Latin America to European producers.

The comments of United States manufacturers to the National Industrial Conference Board are consistent with this hypothesis. The manufacturers claim that their competition in

Europe comes from other European countries and, in less-developed countries, from the Europeans, Australians, and Japanese, where no local production exists. They seldom mention competition from other less-developed countries. Typical is the comment:

Increased competition comes from different major sources and is due in large part to specific situations existing in each country, e.g.:

France -- Local and other European manufacturers are main competition here.

United Kingdom -- Local manufacturers are main competition in U.K.

Australia -- Main competition here is from British and European manufacturers and to a lesser extent Japanese.

Brazil -- Main competition comes from European sources. But local competition is a growing factor here. (A metal working machinery company)[24]

---

24. This and other statements are found in "Foreign Markets: More Important, More Competitive," in the Conference Board Record, March 1965, Vol. 11, No. 3, pp. 17-20.

82

In addition, the low quality version of the product may find a market in segments of the United States population which have been ignored by the United States manufacturer. For example, German and Japanese refrigerators are used in camping vehicles and in summer houses in the United States. The small foreign sedan is typically bought by students, young couples, faculty, or as a second car. An "order of acquisition" concept[25] could lead to the conclusion that the second car or camping refrigerator may be a low-income purchase, made out of the last increments of disposable income left after the acquisition of higher priority items.

As the foreign market grows in income, the products of the higher-income foreign markets become more sophisticated, and foreign producers in other countries begin to compete in world markets. We find, for example, that the Volkswagen "beetle" has moved from 1100 to 1300 cc., from 34 h. p. to 50 h. p. Its market position in Germany has still deteriorated in favor of the more sophisticated Volkswagen 1500 and 1600's. Simultaneously, Japanese vehicles have entered the world markets and are beginning to make inroads into the lower-income countries.

---

25. See Paroush, Jacob: "The Order of Acquisition of Durable Goods, " in Bank of Israel Bulletin, No. 20, Jerusalem, December 1963, pp. 56-73.

There is an interesting related controversy in Great Britain as to the advantages of producing less-orthodox cars, like the Minis or Triumph 1300. The subsidiaries of the American "big three" argue that a conventional car is more suited to the export markets of the United Kingdom. Even if less-developed countries demand local assembly, exports of sub-assemblies will continue from the United Kingdom if the products produced there are suited to the markets of the less-developed countries, or so goes the argument. [26]

Of course, there is no guarantee that a particular foreign producer will become a competitor for the American in third markets. If production in the foreign market is so divided among many producers, perhaps by tacit agreement, that none attains real scale-economies, they will be no threat in third markets. The case of refrigerator manufacture in France offers a good example. The largest producer (Thomson-Houston) builds less than 200,000 units per year and Frigidaire, the second largest, makes only 135,000. One Italian manufacturer alone makes about as many refrigerators per year as the entire French industry (about 1 million). The French imported about 500,000 units in

---

26. See "Car Design: Do It Yourself," The Economist, November 6, 1965, p. 643.

1965, about 60% of which came from Italy. [27]   However, too
little competition caused by protection from high tariffs can also
reduce competitiveness in the world market. The Economist
cites the case of Lucas in England which is described as being in
such a position. [28]

Nationality of the Overseas Producer

Up to this point, it has been assumed that the producer who
starts abroad is a national of that country. In actuality, he may
be a subsidiary of an American producer. One of the dozens of
examples of a United States firm's manufacturing lower-income
products abroad is the case of Burroughs, which plans to make
advanced computers in the United States and conventional equipment in Europe.

The American may try to protect his export markets by
producing locally to preclude a foreigner from doing the same.
Many factors are, of course, important in determining whether
an American makes an overseas investment. It is possible that
he must be in an oligopolistic position in order to be able to pro-

---

27. The Economist, January 8, 1966, pp. 122-124.

28. The Economist, "Cars and their Components," Supplement
     October 23, 1965, pp. viii-x.

tect a market against competitors. In fact, this is probably
the explanation of Stephen Hymer's finding that American investment abroad is concentrated in oligopolistic industries.[29]

The pattern of trade resulting from the introduction of
a new, high-income product in the United States, exports from
the United States, and finally competition from foreign producers or American plants located abroad can be represented
in diagrams. The effects of the variables which have been discussed can be demonstrated graphically.

THE TRADE CYCLE

The previous sections have described a trade cycle for
certain types of large scale manufactured goods. Items which
can be classified as "high-income" will be first produced in the
United States. The United States will export these products to
high-income segments of foreign markets. Eventually, a foreign
market will reach an income-level such that the market size is

29. Hymer, Stephen H., op. cit.; see also Bain, Joe S.,
    Barriers to New Competition, Harvard University Press,
    Cambridge, 1956, for a listing of the possible competitive
    advantages which a firm may have.

large enough that a local producer can attain sufficient scale-
economies with this tariff, transportation, and factor cost
savings that he can underprice the high production volume
products from the United States. Eventually he will gain
sufficient scale economies that he can make inroads into United
States export markets in third countries. Finally, he may export to the United States.

If the foreigner has introduced a lower-quality version
of the product, he may quickly gain low-income or secondary
markets in the United States which have been neglected by the
American producer. In this case, his products also may be
even better suited for third countries.

As incomes grow in this foreign country, the product
becomes more sophisticated and lower-quality items are introduced in other foreign countries.

The United States exports of the product over time should
follow the pattern in Figure II-1. The cycles would have different
amplitudes and durations depending on differences in income-
appeals, transportation and tariff costs, and scale-economies.

If, for example, two products were identical in every respect except that one was purchased primarily by high-income
consumers, the United States exports should continue for a longer

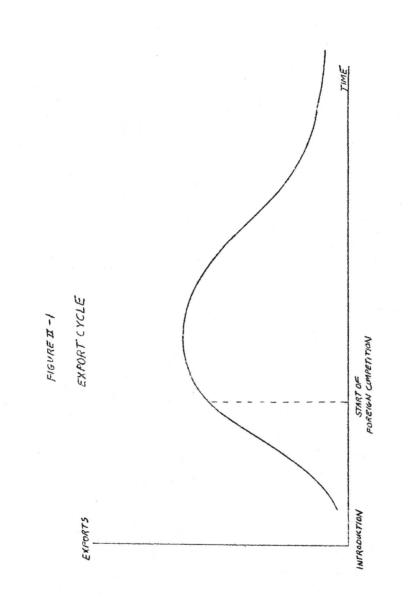

FIGURE II – 1

EXPORT CYCLE

period of time, because a foreign market must grow to a higher
income level before a plant based on the local market can compete with imports from the United States. For these two otherwise identical products, the volume of United States exports
would be the same at the time demand in some country is great
enough that foreign production is introduced (See Figure II-2).
If the change in exports over a period of time is measured, the
exports of the high-income product should decline less than those
of the low income product, as long as the period does not start
immediately after the time of introduction, before any foreign
competition starts, or near the end of the cycle where exports
have become stable.

If two products are considered for which the transportation
and tariff costs were the only differences, the model would predict that the United States exports of the product with lower transportation and duties would reach a higher-volume before foreign
competition starts. The potential foreign producer would receive
less protection to initiate local production (See Figure II-3).

If two products are identical except for returns-to-scale,
the hypothesis says that the product with greater returns-to-scale
should reach a higher level of exports from the United States and
the exports should be maintained longer (See Figure II-4). Con-

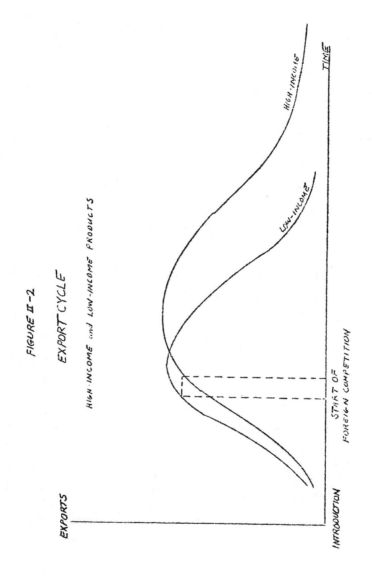

FIGURE II-2

EXPORT CYCLE

HIGH-INCOME and LOW-INCOME PRODUCTS

EXPORTS

HIGH-INCOME

LOW-INCOME

TIME

INTRODUCTION

START OF
FOREIGN COMPETITION

FIGURE II -3

EXPORT CYCLE

PRODUCTS WITH DIFFERENT TARIFFS and TRANSPORTATION

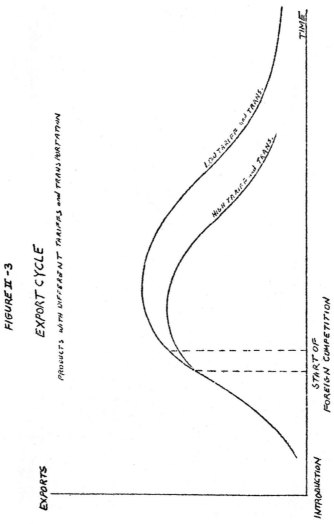

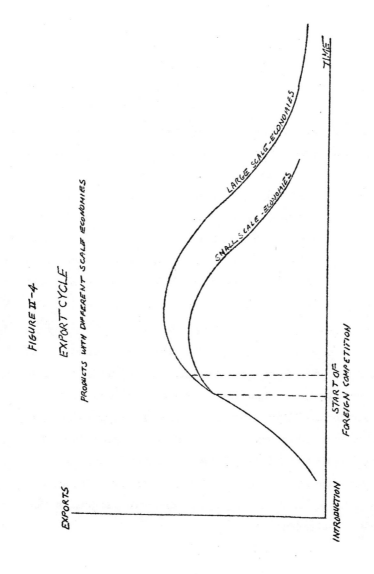

FIGURE II-4

EXPORT CYCLE

PRODUCTS WITH DIFFERENT SCALE ECONOMIES

LARGE SCALE-ECONOMIES

SMALL SCALE-ECONOMIES

EXPORTS

TIME

INTRODUCTION

START OF
FOREIGN COMPETITION

sider, for example, refrigerators and refrigerator compressors.
The demand for the two is identical if we ignore the replacement
parts market. However, the production volume required for low
cost manufacture of compressors is much larger than that required
for low cost assembly of refrigerators. If tariff and transportation
costs were identical, the volume of exports of compressors should
be higher, and last longer, than for completed refrigerators, because the market size required for efficient production of compressors is larger. In fact, this pattern does occur, and countries
often have different tariffs for components than for assembled items
(assembly is often less sensitive to scale) in order to counteract
this phenomenon.

If two products were identical in every respect except for
their time of introduction, the model would predict that they would
have the same trade patterns. The foreign demand for the second
product at its time of introduction, or very soon thereafter, is the
same as for the first product at that time, if they actually appeal
identically to the various income groups (See Figure II-5). If
changes in United States export performance were measured,
then the same results for the two products should be found as
long as the period did not begin too near the date of introduction
of the second product.

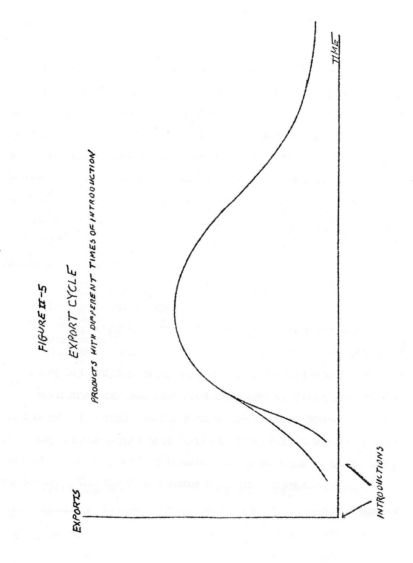

FIGURE II-5

EXPORT CYCLE

PRODUCTS WITH DIFFERENT TIMES OF INTRODUCTION

EXPORTS

TIME

INTRODUCTIONS

If the second product is introduced very late in the cycle of the first, the United States would not be expected to have an export advantage. The product is no longer high-income relative to other products and other markets. Foreign markets are large enough to support efficient production. Witness the previously mentioned case of the stainless-steel razor blade.

Of course, two products are never exactly alike in every respect but one. The next chapter will attempt to isolate some of these effects to see if evidence of their operation can be found.

An Exception to the Cycle Model

One exception to the cycle is the case of very high-income products, for which the total United States market is not large enough to obtain significant scale-economies. In fact, if the choice of technology is not a continuum, unit costs may stay relatively high and constant over a wide range of output. Only at a very large volume is there a rather sudden decrease in cost as another form of technology is introduced.

For such high-income products, production is often decentralized, close to market clusters. The product is usually manufactured to varying specifications. Ship construction probably provides a good example. Other examples are probably high-

performance sports cars (Ferrari's, Aston Martin's, etc.),
and sailboats. With growth in the United States market, these
products may eventually move into the pattern of the previously
described cycle. There is evidence that high-performance sports
cars (Corvette) and sailboats (fibreglass) may already be moving
into this stage.

CHAPTER III

AN EMPIRICAL TEST

This chapter will present the results of an empirical test of the hypothesis. The test will consist of three parts: an examination to see if United States exports of products with varying appeals to income groups do perform significantly differently as predicted; an attempt to see if there is a relationship between scale economies and export performance; and, finally, an examination of transportation costs and tariffs to see if they appear to offer protection to foreign producers.

THE SAMPLE

We have chosen to look at United States exports of consumer durables. Maizels has offered the following definition of consumer durables for a study which he conducted:

> The term is used here to cover passenger road vehicles--passenger cars, motorcycles and bicycles--and those household durables produced by the metal and engineering industries. [1]

We will use this definition, with the addition of recreational watercraft, which were excluded by Maizels.

---

1. Maizels, op. cit., p. 15.

It is generally agreed that consumer durables have significant returns-to-scale[2] and that income is a prime determinant of ownership.[3]

In addition to having scale economies and to being sensitive to income levels, consumer durables offer other advantages. United States export data are available for a large number of rather finely classified "products." Data exist, for example, for refrigerators, freezers, and air conditioners,

---

2. Ibid., p. 22. Maizels divides consumer durables into two groups, "the traditional household goods, such as kitchenware, which can easily be produced in small factories or by artisans, and the newer products of large-scale mechanical and electrical engineering." All of the products which we will be studying are in this second category.

3. See Ibid., p. 22. "In general it appears that income is the main determinant of ownership, but that there are a large number of other factors."

See also, Sultan, op. cit., p. 459. "Until a saturation level is reached, ownership is directly related to household income."

Later in this chapter, we will calculate the income-elasticity of ownership for the products in our sample. The correlation measures will give us an idea of how strong a determinant of ownership income is.

not just for an aggregate classification "refrigeration equipment." Moreover, a great deal of data are available as to who purchases various consumer durables. It is possible to establish the relative income appeal of the different durables. In addition, there are variations in quality within a particular product class which make it possible to look at the relative competitiveness of the United States and other countries for different qualities of the same "product". United States price data and German data for refrigerators and household freezers of different cubic foot capacity can be compared, for example.

Consumer durables offer one other advantage. High-income durables are not necessarily associated with a significantly more advanced technology. Home air conditioners are not more difficult to produce than home freezers or refrigerators. Any European country which can build automobiles can certainly manufacture electric toothbrushes and electric dishwashers, both of which are high-income products. If the United States export performance is different for these products, the cause must be something other than a "technological gap."

Choice of Sample

The list of specific consumer durables to be studied was arrived at by first taking all of the consumer durables included in

the 1961 Starch Consumer Survey questionnaires[4] (See Table
III-1). This list was compared with the Schedule B classifications for United States exports. Those products not included on both lists were eliminated. The elimination of
products not included on the Schedule B list probably caused
the loss of very new items for which a classification had not
yet been introduced.[5] According to the hypothesis, some of
these new products would probably show a rapid rate of growth
in exports.

Each product was assigned a two or three letter code
name for ease of identification. Table III-2 gives the list of
products which remained, the corresponding Schedule B and
SITC group numbers, and the code letters which will be used
to identify the products.

Time Period

Choosing the time period to study the United States export
performance involved two problems: the length of the time period,
and the year with which it would begin or end.

---

4. A survey of 26,317 people in the United States, by Daniel
   Starch and Associates.

5. See, for example, Stobaugh, Robert B., "A Note on Organic
   Chemicals and the Terms of Trade," unpublished. A
   separate classification is introduced only when trade
   becomes large.

Table III-1

Durables Included in 1961-1962 Starch Consumer
Survey Questionnaires

Automobile
Electric mixer
Electric toaster
Electric iron
Electric coffee maker
Electric frypan or skillet
Electric can opener
Refrigerator
Range
Freezer
Electric dishwasher
Electric garbage disposer
Washing machine
Clothes dryer
Television set
Radio
Record playing equipment
Room air conditioner
Vacuum cleaner
Electric floor polisher
Electric bed covering
Electric clock
Movie camera
Movie projector
Still camera
Slide projector
Boat
Outboard Motor

Table III-2

Trade Data Classifications and Code Letters

Product	Schedule B Number	SITC Group	Code Letters
Outboard Motor	71482, 714220[*]	714	OTB
8^{mm} Movie Camera	90015	861	MVC
Still Camera	90030 + 90050	861	STC
Slide Projector	90090	861	SLP
Passenger Car	79070+79075, 790763+790773[*]	732	AUT
Electric Mixer	7071	725	MIX
Electric Iron	70710	725	IR
Refrigerator	70580, 705715[*]	725	REF
Range	70720+61423, 614310[*]	697, 725	RAN
Household Freezer	70585, 705725[*]	725	FRE
Dishwasher	70695	719	DWR
Washing machine	70684+70680, 706814+706812[*]	725	WSR
Clothes Dryer	70688[**]	725	DRR
Television	70815, 707721[*]	724	TV
Radio	70803+70807, 707705+707719[*]	724	RAD
Record Players	92360	891	REC
Room Air Conditioner	76571	719	ARC
Vacuum Cleaner	70691	725	VAC
Electric Clock	95700	864	ECL
Recreational Watercraft	79540, 795150[*]	735	BOT

[*]1952, 1953 data

[**]No classification existed in 1952 and 1953

Source of Schedule B Classifications: U. S. Dept. of Commerce,
Schedule B: Statistical Classification of Domestic & Foreign
Commodities Exported from the United States, U. S. Government Printing Office, Washington, D. C., 1957.

The period needed to be long enough to make sure that changes in export performance could occur, and short enough such that products would not have gone through a complete cycle and such that tariff and transportation costs did not vary greatly. An examination of the export figures led to the belief that a ten year period would be reasonable.

The latest data available were for 1963. This would have meant using 1953 as the starting point, or 1952 if two-year averages of exports at the beginning and end of the period were taken to reduce the chances of giving too much importance to particularly bad or good years. 1952 seemed to be long enough after the immediately post-war years to be satisfactory. In fact, the United Nations makes calculations for 1950-1962 for its latest ten-year terms of trade figures. [6]

The average of 1962 and 1963 exports and the average of 1952 and 1953 exports were taken to calculate increases and decreases in United States exports. The ratio of 1962-1963 average exports to 1952-1953 average exports was calculated for each of the products.

---

6. World Economic Survey, 1962, Part I, United Nations, 1963.

Two adjustments were made to the data. Electric freezers
was the only case in which exports to Canada accounted for more
than 50% of total United States exports and for which the exports
to Canada behaved very differently from those to the rest of the
world. [7] Hence, exports to Canada were eliminated from the
United States export figures for freezers.

The second adjustment was to the fixed-focus still camera
category. The 1963 exports were drastically out of line with the
previous years. Hence, only the 1962 exports were taken. [8]

Table III-3 gives the average exports for the two periods
by value and by number of units. Table III-4 gives the adjusted
ratio of the 1962-1963 exports to the 1952-1953 exports calculated
by units and by value.

7. U.S. Exports of Home Electric Freezers

Year	1952	1962
Total (Units)	21,776	31,093
To Canada (Units)	15,720	9,463
Total (Value)	$4,921,315	$5,200,909
To Canada (Value)	$3,565,622	$1,604,394

8. 1963 exports were 986,018 units as compared to 301,052 for
1962 and 186,526 for 1958.

Table III-3

U. S. Exports for 1952-1953 and 1962-1963[*]

Item	Avg Exports (Units) 1952-1953	Avg Exports (Value) 1952-1953	Avg Exports (Units) 1962-1963	Avg Exports (Value) 1962-1963
OTB	17,578	$2,974,643	50,507	$13,884,016
MVC	14,011	510,444	72,387	2,114,730
STC	132,233	636,455	481,762	3,193,262
SLP	28,528	644,059	44,861	3,009,385
AUT	152,010	266,170,998	144,577	263,809,335
MIX	169,126	2,594,961	219,254	3,242,585
IR-	156,859	911,027	267,066	1,420,393
REF	368,519	60,404,435	171,149	28,099,939
RAN	91,137	7,886,776	71,911	6,872,928
FRE	30,985	6,946,355	31,112	5,144,769
DWR	3,250	634,734	34,435	5,400,979
WSR	70,523	8,054,595	84,683	10,837,494
DRR	n. a.	n. a.	17,136	1,792,418
TV-	100,311	17,157,850	141,698	17,855,756
RAD	122,660	3,091,395	159,183	4,833,637
REC	40,619	1,060,229	46,526	1,922,529
ARC	30,231	7,818,319	148,627	28,090,973
VAC	40,981	1,684,168	88,661	3,001,591
ECL	195,953	' 987,120	197,652	1,025,511
BOT	1,956	1,933,667	4,259	8,508,879

[*]For adjustments, see text.

Source: Calculated from U. S. Dept. of Commerce, Bureau of the Census, United States Exports of Domestic and Foreign Merchandise, Commodity by Country of Destination, FT 410, U. S. Government Printing Office, Washington, D. C., 1952, 1953, 1962, 1963.

Table III-4

Ratio of 1962-1963 Average Exports to 1952-1953 Average Exports

Item	Ratio (Units)	Ratio (Value)
OTB	2.88	4.18
MVC	5.17	4.14
STC	3.65	4.66
SLP	1.57	4.66
AUT	0.95	0.99
MIX	1.29	1.25
IR-	1.71	1.56
REF	0.46	0.47
RAN	0.79	0.87
FRE	3.41	2.65
DWR	10.58	3.50
WSR	1.20	1.35
DRR	n.a.	n.a.
RAD	1.30	1.42
TV-	1.29	1.04
REC	1.12	1.81
ARC	4.60	3.59
VAC	2.07	1.78
ECL	1.01	1.04
BOT	2.17	4.40

UNITED STATES EXPORTS AND THE INCOME-NATURE
OF THE PRODUCT

Necessity, Discretionary, and Luxury Products

If the hypothesis presented in the last chapter is true, United States exports of those products appealing more to a higher-income group should have increased, as compared to those products with an appeal to all groups. One way of classifying the products by appeal is to separate them into necessity, discretionary, and luxury goods; a convenient method for classifying durables and a list of items so classified is given in "The Take-Off Phenomenon. "[9] The approach assumes that ownership of a consumer durable when plotted against household income gives an "S" curve.

---

9. Gately, James, Stephen Gudeman and George Moseley, "The Take-off Phenomenon, " an unpublished paper submitted to Consumer Behavior Research Seminar, Harvard Business School, May 27, 1965.

   See also, Bauer, Raymond A., with Gately, Gudeman, and Moseley, "The 'Take-Off' Phenomenon: A Technique of Market Analysis, " a mimeographed paper.

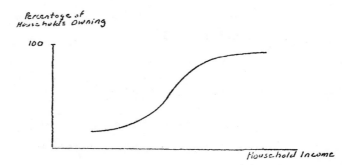

However, when ownership data is actually plotted, three types of curves seem to appear, according to the authors.

The authors argue that these are all really "S" curves, but that they have been shifted to the right or left.

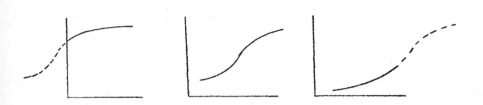

Products having the first curve are called necessity products. These are said to be the products which all households feel that they must have. The second are discretionary. Above a certain income level, called the "take-off point", the product becomes highly desirable. The third are luxury products. Only a small percentage of households own them and no "take-off point" seems to have been reached. The authors argue that products move from luxury to discretionary to necessity over time. Although we have no statistical verification of the approach[10], the method is

10. It would be interesting to test for the "S" curve by fitting to the original data an equation of the form:

$$Y = A \frac{C_2 X^2}{1 + C_1 X + C_2 X^2}$$

where A is the limit approached as X becomes infinitely large. See Zentler, A. P., and Dorothy Ryde, "An Optimum Geographical Distribution of Publicity Expenditure in a Private Organization," Management Service, July 1956, pp. 337-352, for a discussion of this type of curve.

convenient and yields a list which is intuitively acceptable.
Table III-5 gives Gately, Gudeman, and Moseley's classification of products which are in our sample.

Assuming no other systematic differences, the ratio of
1962-1963 to 1952-1953 average exports should be higher for
luxury goods than for discretionary goods, which should, in
turn, be higher than for necessity products. Table III-6 gives
the average ratio for the products in each group, by value and
by quantity. The increase in exports was highest for luxury
products and lowest for necessity products as predicted. Snede-
cor's "F" was calculated for both sets of data and was found
to be significant at the .01 level in both cases. Table III-7 shows
a similar calculation made without the adjustment for Canadian
freezers. On the uncorrected data, the results are significant
at better than the .05 level for the value ratio and just miss
significance at the .05 level for the quantity ratio.

It is fairly safe, then, to assume that the differences did
not arise by chance. The data do indeed seem to be in agreement
with the hypothesis.

Table III-5

Classification of Products by Necessity, Discretionary, Luxury

Necessity

REF   IR-
RAN   TV-
RAD

Discretionary

AUT   VAC
ECL   MIX
STC   REC
WSR

Luxury

DRR   SLP
MVC   DWR
FRE   OTB
ARC   BOT

Source: Gateley, Gudeman, Moseley, op. cit., Exhibit C.

Table III-6

Ratio of 1962-1963 Exports to 1952-1953 Exports
for Necessity, Discretionary, and Luxury Products

By Value

Necessity		Discretionary		Luxury	
REF	0.47	AUT	0.99	MVC	4.14
RAN	0.87	ECL	1.04	FRE	2.65
RAD	1.42	STC	4.66	ARC	3.59
IR	1.56	WSR	1.35	SLP	4.66
TV	1.04	VAC	1.78	DWR	8.50
		MIX	1.25	OTB	4.13
		REC	1.81	BOT	4.40
Av.	1.07		1.84		4.59

$F = 11.5$

By Units

Necessity		Discretionary		Luxury	
REF	0.46	AUT	0.95	MVC	5.17
RAN	0.79	ECL	1.01	FRE	3.41
RAD	1.30	STC	3.65	ARC	4.60
IR	1.71	WSR	1.20	SLP	1.57
TV	1.29	VAC	2.07	DWR	10.58
		MIX	1.29	OTB	2.88
		REC	1.12	BOT	2.17
Av.	1.11		1.61		4.34

$F = 6.3$

Table III-7

Ratio of 1962-1963 Exports to 1952-1953 Exports for Necessity,
Discretionary, and Luxury Products
Unadjusted for Exports of Freezers to Canada

By Value

Necessity		Discretionary		Luxury	
REF	0.47	AUT	0.99	MVC	4.14
RAN	0.87	ECL	1.04	FRE	0.74
RAD	1.42	STC	4.66	ARC	3.59
IR	1.56	WSR	1.35	SLP	4.66
TV	1.04	VAC	1.78	DWR	8.50
		MIX	1.25	OTB	4.18
		REC	1.81	BOT	4.40
Av.	1.07		1.84		4.32

$F = 7.0$

By Units

Necessity		Discretionary		Luxury	
REF	0.46	AUT	0.95	MVC	5.17
RAN	0.79	ECL	1.01	FRE	1.01
RAD	1.30	STC	3.65	ARC	4.60
IR	1.71	WSR	1.20	SLP	1.57
TV	1.29	VAC	2.07	DWR	10.58
		MIX	1.29	OTB	2.88
		REC	1.12	BOT	2.17
Av.	1.11		1.61		4.00

$F = 3.4$

Ownership Elasticity and "Saturation"

Quantitatively measurable characteristics of the products
may also be used to describe "income-nature." Two characteristics of the income-ownership curve allowed Gately, Gudeman,
and Moseley to classify their products; the height of the curve,
i. e. the "saturation," or overall percentage of households owning the durable, and the rate of increase in ownership with an increase in income. The first measure is easy to calculate by
taking the number of households owning the item as a fraction of
the number of households responding. The second measure is
easier if it is recognized that the curves are very close to linear
on log-log paper, i. e., that the percentage increase in ownership
per percentage increase in income is almost constant over the
range of incomes included. The slope of this straight line on log-
log paper is the income-elasticity of ownership.

Table III-8 shows the number of households owning at least
one of the durable, the number of households responding, and the
ratio of these two numbers, or the degree of "saturation." Of
course, this number can be greater than 1.0 if multiple ownership is taken into account. For those products for which the information was available, the total number of the items owned was

115

Table III-8

Fraction of Households Owning Each Durable

Item	Number Owning Divided by Number of Respondents
OTB	.084
MVC	.132
STC	.656
SLP	.096
AUT	.756
MIX	.670
IR	.968
REF	.984
RAN	.988
FRE	.194
DWR	.051
WSR	.748
DRR	.191
RAD	.986
TV	.902
REC	.501
ARC	.105
VAC	.735
ECL	.747
BOT	.006
AUT NO	.940
RAD NO	1.678
TV NO	1.405
REC NO	.578

Source: Calculated from ADLTAB Print-out from Starch Consumer Survey.

divided by the number of respondents. It will be noted that this number is available for those items where multiple ownership is likely to be very significant. Where multiple ownership is included, the product designation is followed by a "NO".

The second measure, the rate of increase of ownership with an increase in income may be calculated by finding the "b" in the following equation:

log fraction of households in each income group owning = a + b · log household income

The data divided the households into eight income groups:

Group	Yearly Income
1	under $2,000
2	$2,000 - 2,999
3	$3,000 - 3,999
4	$4,000 - 4,999
5	$5,000 - 6,999
6	$7,000 - 9,999
7	$10,000 - 14,999
8	$15,000 and over

The average income for each group of households was assumed to be at the midpoint in the range, with Group 1 at $1,000 and Group 8 at $16,000. The least-squares method was used to calculate the income-elasticity of ownership for each product. The resultant elasticities and R^2's are shown in Table III-9. The other

Table III-9

Income-Elasticity of Ownership

Product	Elasticity	R^2
OTB	0.886	.843
MVC	1.432	.925
STC	0.553	.922
SLP	1.526	.982
AUT	0.457	.875
MIX	0.382	.939
IR	0.042	.867
REF	0.032	.756
RAN	0.020	.655
FRE	0.463	.963
DWR	2.112	.931
WSR	0.157	.779
DRR	1.248	.953
RAD	0.091	.942
TV	0.147	.872
REC	0.642	.953
ARC	0.908	.952
VAC	0.342	.910
ECL	0.214	.871
BOT	0.823	.927
AUT NO	0.620	.980
RAD NO	0.427	.926
TV NO	0.269	.986
REC NO	0.729	.962

characteristics of the regression equations are included in the
Appendix. It is worth noting that twenty out of the twenty-four
R^2's are above .850, i. e., in twenty cases out of the twenty-
four, the linear transformation of income explained 85% of the
variance in the average rate of ownership in the different income
groups.

Before the association between United States export performance and these measures of the income-nature of the products is examined, it is necessary to look at some of the problems
associated with the measures. Three types of problems occur:

1. The data are cross-sectional instead of time-series

2. United States data are used instead of some sort of international data, and

3. Income-elasticities sometimes have strange characteristics.

For example, they are sometimes negative at high-incomes and
they sometimes change over time. Each of these problems will
be examined separately. Although not all the weaknesses can be
removed, there seem to be no systematic errors that would cause
the data to confirm the hypothesis.

Since the data are cross-sectional instead of time-series,
they may not represent what is being sought. The measures
should indicate what happens to ownership of the durables as in-

comes grow. The hypothesis was that as foreign incomes grow, foreigners would purchase more of American high-income goods. The data should measure the rate of growth of their purchases. Time-series data are difficult to come by, and when they are available, they are fraught with problems. Prices change over time, so it is difficult to separate the changes in ownership due to changes in price from those associated with changes in income. Secondly, income-elasticity changes over time, a problem which will be discussed later. It is, thus fairly common to take cross-sectional data as a substitute for time-series data. [11] Cross-sectional data is certainly not perfect, but that it is probably a reasonable reflection of the relative rankings of what one would obtain from time-series data is recognized. Over a relatively short period of time, cross-sectional data does probably reflect the changes in behavior as households move from one income-group to the next.

Another problem with the measures of the income-appeal of products is that they are based solely on United States data. If the data were available, the rate of increase in the rest of the world's consumption over time would be taken. The consumption of each item will not be growing at the same rate in each country. There are also other factors than income which affect consumption.

---

11. For a comparison of results using cross-sectional and time-series data for various characteristics of consumer durables, see Sultan, Ralph, op. cit., Chapter VI.

For example, the Norwegians would probably not have as many
air conditioners as the Kuwaitis, even if their incomes were the
same. The diversity of the United States market does give
reason to believe that it might reflect fairly well the consumption patterns of at least the rest of the industrialized world,
which is the primary export market for consumer durables.

In order to test this assertion, consumption patterns in
the United Kingdom and in the European Economic Community
were compared with American patterns. A Reader's Digest
study[12] gave comparable data for the United States, the United
Kingdom, and the European Economic Community (See Table
III-10). A ranking of the degree of saturation in the three areas
gave a way of measuring the similarities in the patterns. "W",
the Coefficient of Concordance, was calculated for the rankings.
The results for the products in the Reader's Digest study and in
this study are shown in Table III-11. "W" is .905. Perfect
agreement would have yielded 1.000, so the degree of similarity
in ownership patterns is very high. The sharp-eyed reader will
note a slight difference in the ranking of the first three products
in this study and in the previous data. This difference can be

----

12. The European Common Market and Britain, Basic Report,
     Reader's Digest Association, Inc., 1963.

Table III-10

Ownership of Consumer Durables in the United States, the
European Economic Community and Great Britain

Percent of Households Owning

Product:	AUT	AUT[*]	TV	RAD	REC	REF	VAC	MIX	DWR	IR	MVC
E. E. C.	28	1	34	79	28	40	42	21	-	81	2
G. B.	32	3	82	76	39	30	72	5	-	91	2
U. S.	77	18	90	91	50	96	73	69	6	97	13

[*]Two or more cars

Source: The European Common Market and Britain, Basic Report,
Reader's Digest Association, Inc., 1963.

Table III-11

Ranking of Ownership in U. S., U. K., and E. E. C.

Product:	IR	REF	RAD	TV	AUT	VAC	MIX	REC	AUT[*]	MVC	DWR
Rank in U. S.	11	10	9	8	7	6	5	4	3	2	1
Rank in U. K.	11	5	9	10	6	8	4	7	3	2	1
Rank in E. E. C.	11	8	10	7	5.5	9	4	5.5	2	3	1

W = Coefficient of Concordance[**] = .905

[*] 2 or more automobiles

[**] For method of computation, see Moroney, M. J., Facts from Figures, Penguin Books, Baltimore, 1951, pp. 337-338.

attributed, no doubt, to the quite different sampling techniques and to the closeness of these three numbers to each other within a country. The agreement among the three geographical areas is almost perfect in the items with low saturation, and where the differences in saturation are larger.

Another interesting measure with the ownership figures is the degree of lead of the United States over lower-income countries. If the low-saturation products are the most highly-elastic (as was observed from the U. S. data), the United States, as a higher-income country, might be expected to be further in the lead in ownership of lower-saturation items. A comparison of the ranking of the products by saturation in the United States with the ranking by the ratio of E. E. C. saturation to U. S. saturation provides a test for this hypothesis. The results shown in Table III-12 show that the Spearman's Rank Correlation Coefficient is . 71, which is significant at the . 05 level. The same table gives the result of ranking the United States income-elasticity of ownership against the ratio of E. E. C. saturation to U. S. saturation. In this case, the Spearman's

Table III-12

Relative Lead of the United States in High Saturation and Low Saturation Products

Product	Rank by Saturation in U. S.	Rank by Ratio of E. E. C. Saturation to U.S. Saturation
IR	1	2
REF	2	5
RAD	3	1
TV	4	6
AUT	5	7
VAC	6	3
MIX	7	8
REC	8	4
MVC	9	9
DWR	10	10

Spearman's Coefficient = . 71

Product	Rank by U. S. Income-Elasticity of Ownership	Rank by Ratio of E. E. C. Saturation to U.S. Saturation
IR	2	2
REF	1	5
RAD	3	1
TV	4	6
AUT	7	7
VAC	5	3
MIX	6	8
REC	8	4
MVC	9	9
DWR	10	10

Spearman's Coefficient = . 71

Coefficient is also .71. The United States data do seem to be a fair reflection of ownership patterns at least in Western Europe, and the elasticity does appear to reflect to some extent the relative difference in ownership levels between the United States and Europe for a particular product.

In addition, there is some reason to believe that the United States data are not bad reflections of ownership patterns in other parts of the world. Jacob Paroush's calculations of the order of acquisition of consumer durables in Israel [13] demonstrate a pattern similar to that in the United States and Western Europe. Paroush ranks the order of acquisition of durables in Israel as radio, gas cooker, refrigerator, washing machine, electric mixer, and vacuum cleaner. The saturation figures for the United States indicate that only the last two items are reversed. It must be noted that Paroush's figures are for "order of acquisition" and not for saturation. However, there does appear to be a great degree of similarity in his results for Israel and those of this study for the United States.

----

13. Paroush, op. cit.

Unfortunately, most of the large studies of household
expenditures for other countries include only aggregate
classes of expenditures (such as food, durables, and clothing,
telling nothing about the patterns within the durables class.
Irving Kravis does say that " the figures indicate that the
degree of similarity in consumption patterns is directly
correlated with the degree of similarity in levels of per
capita income. " [14] Since the previous chapter hypothe-
sized that the United States will be exporting primarily
to the high-income markets, the consumption patterns of
the United States export markets are likely to be similar
to American patterns.

An addition to the appropriateness of cross-sectional
data as opposed to time-series data and to the use of
United States data instead of international data, the
question arose as to the adequacy of the measures of
the income-appeal of the products on two other grounds,
the instability of elasticity measures over time and the
fact that it is possible to get negative elasticities at high
incomes.

14. Kravis, Irving, "Comparisons of the Structure of
Consumption, " in Clark, Lincoln (ed.), Consumer
Behavior: Research in Consumer Reactions, Harper
and Brothers, New York, 1958.

Many new products do have an appeal to a higher-income group initially than they will late in the product cycle. High-income households are more likely to try a new product.[15] In addition, as technology becomes more stable and competition increases, prices will generally fall, making the product more attractive to lower-income families. Although it would be interesting to test the stability of our measures over a period of several years, it must be noted that none of the products in the sample is extremely new. Moreover, the newest are probably those showing the highest elasticity at the end of the period. If the elasticities had been measured for 1952, they would probably have been even higher for these products. However, it is doubtful that the rankings would have been significantly different.[16]

---

15. See, for example, Bell, William Earl, Consumer Innovation: An Investigation of Selected Characteristics of Innovations, D. B. A. Thesis, Michigan State University, 1962.

16. A comparison with Ralph Sultan's data, op. cit., pp. 34-35, for 1958 gives the same ranking for the highly elastic products which are included in both samples (dishwasher, dryer, air conditioner, and freezer).

The other problem, that of negative elasticities, is
one that does not seem very important for the products
and income-ranges dealt with in this study. A fall-off
in ownership at high-incomes exists only in washing
machines. This fall-off is probably due to a tendency
of very high-income families either to send their laundry
out or to have servants to do it. There are, of course,
many so-called "inferior" products for which the
consumption or ownership does fall off with increased
income. The classic example is potatoes. Durables
falling into this category include motor cycles and
bicycles (See Table III-13 for ownership patterns for
these two items.). If the sample had included such
products and if the level of income at which ownership
begins to decline is less than that of European countries,
the United States would probably not be competitive
(witness the cases of bicycles and motor cycles, both
of which face strong import competition in the United
States).

It seems safe, then, to conclude that the measures
do not contain any systematic errors which should
cause them to support the hypothesis. Cross-sectional

Table III-13

Ownership of "Inferior" Durables

Numbers per 1,000 Population

Country	Motorcycles	Bicycles
Canada	2	31
U.S.	3	143
West Germany	48	315
France	41	190
Argentina	2	205
Japan	6	166

Source: Maizels, op. cit., p. 21.

data seem to be the best data available. Although they
are not equivalent to time-series data, they may provide
a reasonable substitute. The United States data do
seem to provide a good substitute for international figures.
Hence, the data will be used, with the recognition that
they are less than perfect, but any correlation which is
found will probably not be due to systematic errors in
the data.

United States Export Performance, Saturation, and Elasticity

The measures of saturation and elasticity may, then,
be useful to test for a relationship of the income-nature
of products to United States export performance. The
hypothesis predicted that higher-income products would
perform better than lower-income products. According
to the model, products with high-elasticity and low
saturation should have performed better over the period
which is being studied.

Elasticity and saturation were used as predictors of
export performance, by finding the constants for the
following equations:

Let R = Ratio of 1962-1963 exports to 1952-1953 exports,
  by value,

and S_{no} = Ratio of the number of items owned to the number
  of households,

and S = Fraction of households owning at least one of the
  item,

and e = Income-elasticity of ownership.

1. $R = a + b \log 100 \times S_{no}$ Table III-14

2. $R = a + b \log 100 \times S_{no} + c \cdot e$ Table III-15

3. $R = a + b \log 100 \times S + c \cdot e$ Table III-16

4. $R = a + b \cdot e$ Table III-17

5. $R = a + b \cdot e + c \cdot S$ Table III-18

Equation 4 gives the best results for a single independent variable. With elasticity as the predictor of export performance, 80% of the variance in the data is explained ($R = .89$). The F and T tests show significance at far better than the .01 level. The regression coefficient for elasticity is positive, as expected, and equals 3.17.

Adding the saturation as a predictor, gives only a slight reduction in the unexplained variance. In Equation 3,

Table III-14

CORRELATION COEFFICIENT FOR EACH VARIABLE -SQUARED
0.53028436

ORIGINAL MATRIX
0.71684715E 01
-0.17235747E 02

INVERSE MATRIX
0.13949975E 00

COEFFICIENTS
-0.24043824E 01
CONSTANT TERM   0.87449521E 01

TOTAL SUM OF SQUARES   0.74483895E 02
SUM OF SQUARES REMOVED BY REGRESSION   0.41441327E 02
RESIDUAL SUM OF SQUARES   0.33042568E 02

STANDARD ERROR OF ESTIMATE   0.13941594E 01
MULTIPLE CORRELATION COEFFICIENT   0.72820629E 00

F,K,N-K-1
0.21321060E 02,   1,   17

FOR EACH COEFFICIENT

STANDARD ERROR   T
0.52071387E 00   -0.46174733E 01

Table III-15

CORRELATION COEFFICIENT FOR EACH VARIABLE -SQUARED
0.53028436
0.76588016

ORIGINAL MATRIX
0.71684715E 01 -0.42716162E 01
-0.42716162E 01   0.56903778E 01
-0.17235747E 02   0.18169331E 02

INVERSE MATRIX
0.25240528E 00   0.18947397E 00
0.18947397E 00   0.31796836E 00

COEFFICIENTS
-0.90777825E 00
0.25115469E 01
CONSTANT TERM   0.33795222E 01

TOTAL SUM OF SQUARES   0.74483895E 02
SUM OF SQUARES REMOVED BY REGRESSION   0.61279363E 02
RESIDUAL SUM OF SQUARES   0.13204532E 02

STANDARD ERROR OF ESTIMATE   0.90845102E 00
$R =$ MULTIPLE CORRELATION COEFFICIENT   0.89473996E 00

F,K,N-K-1
0.37126261E 02,   2,   16

FOR EACH COEFFICIENT

STANDARD ERROR   T
0.45640536E 00   -0.19889737E 01
0.51226357E 00   0.49028411E 01

133

Table III-16

CORRELATION COEFFICIENT FOR EACH VARIABLE -SQUARED
0.52381327
0.80318811

ORIGINAL MATRIX
0.65882266E 01 -0.44604661E 01
-0.44604661E 01   0.60306344E 01
-0.16432462E 02   0.19123064E 02

INVERSE MATRIX
0.30403347E 00   0.22487369E 00
0.22487369E 00   0.33214440E 00

COEFFICIENTS
-0.69574458E 00
0.26563903E 01
CONSTANT TERM   0.28291674E 01

TOTAL SUM OF SQUARES   0.74483895E 02
SUM OF SQUARES REMOVED BY REGRESSION   0.62231118E 02
RESIDUAL SUM OF SQUARES   0.12252777E 02

STANDARD ERROR OF ESTIMATE   0.87509917E 00
MULTIPLE CORRELATION COEFFICIENT   0.90273741E 00

F,K,N-K-1
0.40631519E 02,   2,   16

FOR EACH COEFFICIENT

STANDARD ERROR   T
0.48252295E 00 -0.14418891E 01
0.50433689E 00   0.52670950E 01

Table III-17

CORRELATION COEFFICIENT FOR EACH VARIABLE —SQUARED
0.80318811

ORIGINAL MATRIX
0.60306344E 01
0.19123064E 02

INVERSE MATRIX
0.16582003E 00

COEFFICIENTS
0.31709870E 01
CONSTANT TERM   0.78398321E 00

TOTAL SUM OF SQUARES   0.74483895E 02
SUM OF SQUARES REMOVED BY REGRESSION   0.60638987E 02
RESIDUAL SUM OF SQUARES   0.13844908E 02

STANDARD ERROR OF ESTIMATE   0.90244465E 00
MULTIPLE CORRELATION COEFFICIENT   0.89620764E 00

F,K,N-K-1
0.74457900E 02,   1,   17

FOR EACH COEFFICIENT

STANDARD ERROR   T
0.36748454E 00   0.86288991E 01

Table III-18

CORRELATION COEFFICIENT FOR EACH VARIABLE -SQUARED
```
                0.80318811
                0.60122780
```

ORIGINAL MATRIX
```
 0.60306344E 01  -0.32323369E 01
-0.32323369E 01   0.25182826E 01
 0.19123064E 02  -0.10813356E 02
```

INVERSE MATRIX
```
 0.53141326E 00   0.68209448E 00
 0.68209448E 00   0.12725971E 01
```

COEFFICIENTS
```
 0.27865192E 01
-0.71730918E 00
CONSTANT TERM      0.13994899E 01
```

```
TOTAL SUM OF SQUARES                      0.74483895E 02
SUM OF SQUARES REMOVED BY REGRESSION      0.61043305E 02
RESIDUAL SUM OF SQUARES                   0.13440590E 02
```

```
STANDARD ERROR OF ESTIMATE                0.91653526E 00
MULTIPLE CORRELATION COEFFICIENT          0.89274531E 00
```

F,K,N-K-1
```
         0.36333706E 02,    2,    16
```

FOR EACH COEFFICIENT

```
STANDARD ERROR              T
 0.66813677E 00   -0.41705820E 01
 0.10339383E 01   -0.69376401E 00
```

the best predictor, the addition of the logarithm of saturation increases the multiple correlation coefficient to
.9027, from the .8962 of elasticity alone.   The coefficient
of the saturation is significant only at the .20 level.   In
20% of the samples from such a universe where saturation
adds nothing to the information, a coefficient as high as
.69 would be found by chance.   It is very possible that the
increase in R is simply by chance.

The coefficient for saturation is negative (Equations 1, 2, 3),
as was predicted, showing that the United States exports
increased for low-saturation items. Figures III-1 and III-2
show graphically the relationship between saturation and
export performance and between elasticity and export
performance. Note that still cameras are far from the
trend line in each graph. No doubt, the 1962 data for
exports is high for another reason.

Of course, the addition of saturation as a variable adds
little because it is highly correlated with elasticity.
Saturation alone explains 53% of the variance (Equation I)
and F and T tests show a large degree of significance
(far above the .01 level).   Figure III-3 shows the relation
of saturation to elasticity.   The relationship for saturation

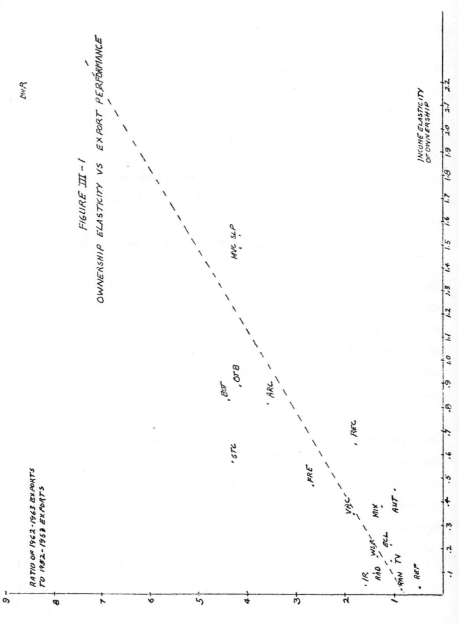

FIGURE III-1

OWNERSHIP ELASTICITY VS EXPORT PERFORMANCE

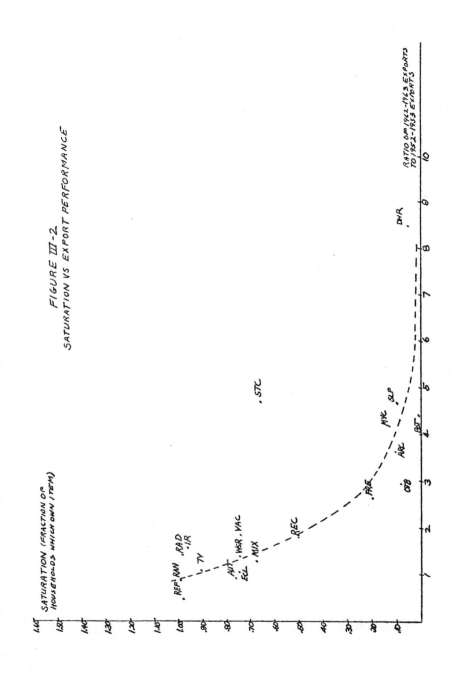

FIGURE III-2

SATURATION VS EXPORT PERFORMANCE

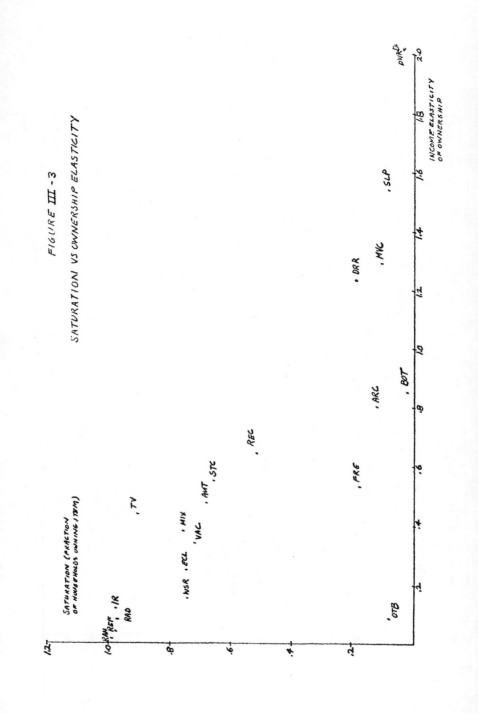

FIGURE III - 3

SATURATION VS OWNERSHIP ELASTICITY

alone to export performance could probably be improved
by using a different function in the regression model.

A strong relationship between degree of ownership,
elasticity, and export performance does exist as was
predicted. The hypothesis said, though, that this relation
would be due to an advantage of the United States in world
trade. The data so far have done nothing to show that the
United States is not just sharing in a more rapid growth
of world trade in high-income products. It is certainly
possible that world trade is growing most rapidly in high-
income items and that the United States is simply keeping
a constant share of world trade in these products.

It is possible to test whether this is an advantage of the
United States or simply a growth with world trade. Maizels'
data[17] for the ratio of 1960 to 1950 world trade in the products
which are included in our sample can be compared to the
performance of United States exports. A positive association
would lead us to believe that the United States is simply

_____ _ _____

17. Maizels, op. cit., Table 10, p. 16.

142

sharing in the growth of world trade. Table III-20 shows
the rankings and the Spearman Rank Correlation Coefficient.
The correlation is negative, although probably not very significant. Hence, it is rather safe to conclude that the figures
show an advantage for the United States in high-income consumer durables in world trade.

It is also interesting to note at this point the performance
of some of the older, lower-income products over a longer
period of time. Prewar tariff and transportation costs
were so different from those of the period under study that
the total export figures may not be very comparable. However, United States automobile exports in 1937 were 231, 482
units and exports of radios were 618, 710, both considerably
larger than the postwar figures in this study.

Even more interesting are the changes in shares of
world exports in the older products, a measure which
takes into account changes in tariffs and transportation.
Table III-21 shows the changes for several products. Note
that the United States market share declined considerably
from 1937 to 1958 for automobiles, washing-machines, and
refrigerators and increased for record players, consistent
with the hypothesis.

Table III-20

United States Share in Growth of World Exports

Product	Rank by Growth[*] in World Trade, 1950 to 1958	Rank by Growth in U.S. Exports, 1952-1953 to 1962-1963
RAD & TV	1	5
REC	2	2
REF	3	8
RAN[**]	4	7
VAC[**]	5	3
WSR	6	4
STC	7	1

Spearman's Coefficient = -.63

[*]Source: Maizels, op. cit., p. 16.

[**]Although these categories were not always identical to ours, they were considered to be close enough.

Table III-21

U. S. Share in World Market, 1937-1958

Product	1937	1958
Passenger cars and chassis	50	13
Electric Washing Machines	98	28
Domestic Refrigerators	67	36
Gramophones, Record Players, Tape Recorders, etc.	5	24

Source: Maizels, op. cit., pp. 29-31.

Quality

In addition to predicting that the United States would
perform better exporting higher-income products, the
model also predicted that the United States would have
an advantage in higher-income versions compared to
lower-income versions of the same product.[18] Because the export data are not broken down finely enough
to test this hypothesis on trade data, prices in several
countries will be compared.

If a product is selected for which the versions may
be ranked from high-quality to low-quality and the
assumption is made that the higher-quality versions
are the higher-income versions, then it is possible to
compare United States prices and foreign prices to test
this hypothesis. The model predicts that the United States
prices should be relatively cheaper for the higher-
quality versions than for the lower-quality ones.
Four products were selected from the sample for which
foreign prices were available and which could be ranked by

18. Of course, the word "product" could be used more
restrictively to apply to each size of an electric
freezer, for example, as a separate "product."
This statement would be no different from our
previous prediction for different products, in this
case.

quality.

Figures III-4 through III-7 show the prices of freezers, refrigerators, electric mixers, and transistor radios in the United States, Germany, and, in some cases, Japan.

Figure III-4, for electric freezers, demonstrates well that the United States prices are lower for high-quality items, that Germany's are lower for middle-quality items, and probably that Japanese prices are lower for low-quality items. The slope of the price-quality line is lowest for the United States, steeper for Germany, and steepest for Japan, showing the comparative advantage of each country. This find is consistent with the hypothesis that the United States has reached large returns-to-scale on the high-quality items, that Germany has returns-to-scale on middle-quality products, and that Japan has scale-economies on low-quality items (See Tables III-22 and III-23).[19] Of course, the production need not be as great for Germany and Japan for the lower-quality items for the prices to be lower. Factor costs are lower. It is only possible to say

19. Tables III-26 and III-27 give measures of the production and consumption of refrigerators by size for Japan and and the United States and production figures for freezers for the United States.

Table III-22

1963 U. S. Production of Refrigerators and Freezers

	1963 Production (Units)
Refrigerators	
8. 4 ft^3 & under	37, 330
8. 5 - 9. 4	47, 014
9. 5 - 10. 4	429, 564
10. 5 - 11. 4	206, 422
11. 5 - 12. 4	922, 572
12. 5 - 13. 4	768, 406
13. 5 - 14. 4	1, 234, 949
14. 5 - 15. 4	147, 099
15. 5 and over	403, 609
Freezers	
8. 4 ft^3 & under	16, 768
8. 5 - 10. 4	56, 570
10. 5 - 12. 4	96, 908
12. 5 - 14. 4	143, 736
14. 5 - 15. 4	224, 627
15. 5 - 17. 4	227, 625
17. 5 - 19. 4	70, 640
19. 5 - 21. 4	99, 732
21. 5 +	101, 007

Source: 1963 Census, Industry Reports, SIC 3632.

Table III-23

Size of Refrigerators in Japan, 1958

	Percent of Units
3.5 cu ft. or smaller	50%
Greater than 3.5 cu ft. but smaller than 5.7 cu ft.	45%
5.7 cu ft. or larger	5%
Total 1958 demand	316,000 units
Total 1962 demand (estimated)	1,273,000 units

Source: Tokai Electric Company, Case written by
    Mr. Shoto Fujieda of the Keio Business School
    LC H 8 M31

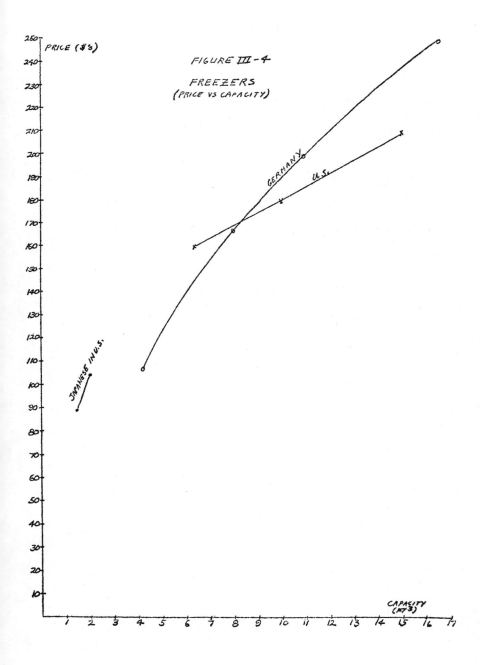

FIGURE III - 4

FREEZERS
(PRICE VS CAPACITY)

Notes to Figure III-4

Prices for U. S. freezers are from the Sears Roebuck Catalog, Fall and Winter, 1965. All prices are for the lowest priced model of the size given.

Prices for German freezers are from the Neckermann Katalog, No. 169, September 1, 1965 - March 1, 1966. Prices are converted at DM 4 = $1, and capacity at 1 cu. ft. = 28.3 ltrs.

Prices for Japanese freezers are from Sears Roebuck Catalog, Spring and Summer, 1966, for Japanese imports.

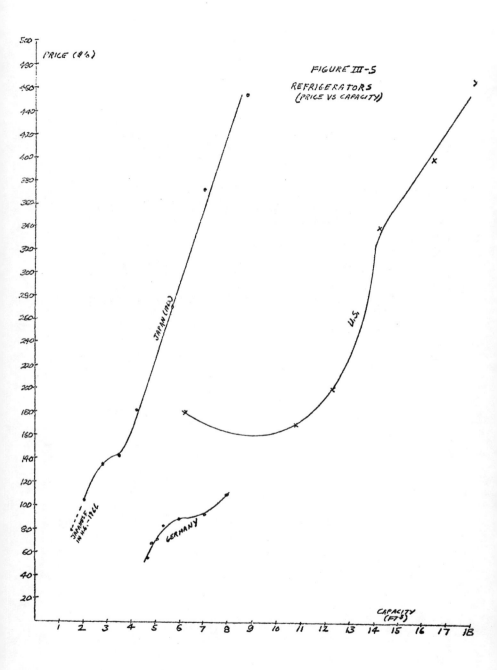

FIGURE III-5

REFRIGERATORS
(PRICE VS CAPACITY)

Notes to Figure III-5

Prices for U. S. refrigerators are from the Sears
Roebuck Catalog, Fall and Winter, 1965, except for
the 6.2 cu. ft. model, which is a locally quoted
discount price for a G. E. model. The next larger
G. E. model is also lower in price, comparable to the
Sears model used.

Prices for German refrigerators are from the Neckermann Kataleg, No. 169, September 1, 1965- March 1,
1966. Prices are converted at DM4 = $1 and capacities
at 1 cu. ft. = 28.3 ltrs.

Prices for the 1.5 cu. ft. and 2 cu. ft. Japanese
freezers are from the Sears Roebuck Catalog, Spring
and Summer, 1966. Prices for the larger Japanese
refrigerators are from "Tokai Electric Company," case
written by Mr. Shoto Fujieda of the Keio Business
School, ICH 8M31, 1962 data. Prices are converted at
Yen 362 = $1.

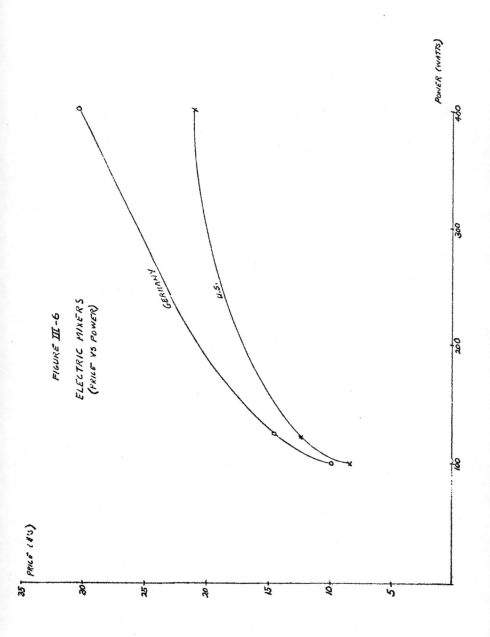

FIGURE III-6

ELECTRIC MIXERS
(PRICE VS POWER)

PRICE ($'s)

POWER (WATTS)

GERMANY

U.S.

154

Notes to Figure III-6

Prices for U. S. mixers are from the <u>Sears Roebuck Catalog</u>, Fall and Winter, 1965

Prices for the German mixers are from the <u>Neckermann Katalog</u>, No. 169, September 1, 1965- March 1, 1966. Prices are converted at DM4 = $1.

Prices were taken for mixers having comparable features for a given motor output.

FIGURE III-7

TRANSISTOR RADIOS
(PRICE VS NO. OF TRANSISTORS)

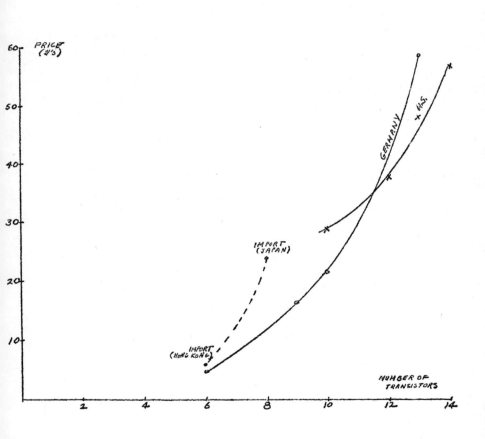

Notes to Figure III-7

Prices for U. S. transistor radios are from the Sears
Roebuck Catalog, Fall and Winter, 1965

Prices for the German transistor radios are from the
Neckermann Katalog, No. 169, September 1, 1965-March1,
1966. Prices are converted at DM4 = $1.

Prices for Japanese and Hong Kong transistor radios are
from the Sears Roebuck Catalog, Fall and Winter, 1965.

Radios were chosen which had similar characteristics
for a given number of transistors (e.g. number of
bands received, number of diodes).

that the volume attained is sufficiently great that, at the lower factor costs, German prices are lower.

The same pattern is repeated in the other illustrations. With the exception of the 1962 prices for refrigerators in Japan, all Japanese prices include tariffs and transportation to the United States. Thus, the absolute level of the curve is distorted, although the slope is probably reasonably accurate.

Note also. that the price for the 6.2 cubic foot refrigerator in the United States is greater than the price for a larger unit. The dealer who provided this price explained that not enough units of this size were sold to enable them to have a lower price. This explanation is consistent with the model proposed.

The data do appear to be in agreement with the hypothesis that the United States will be a relatively cheaper producer of higher-quality versions of a product.

SCALE ECONOMIES

All of the predictions for export performance for products
with differing income-appeals were based on the assumption
of increasing returns-to-scale. Chapter II also predicted
that products which, in some sense, have differing returns-
to-scale would perform differently as exports. Let us look
more into what is meant by differing returns-to-scale.

Consider first two products which have production cost
curves which look like the following for the firm:

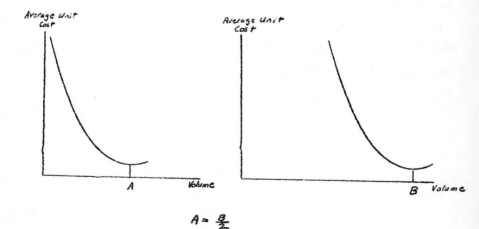

$$A = \frac{B}{2}$$

Assume that, at a given income and price, the demand
in units for each of the items is identical, and that the price-
elasticities are the same.

If the total United States market for each of the products
is B units (or 2A units), then one plant can produce Product II
at lowest unit cost and two plants can produce Product I at
lowest cost. It is more likely that a foreign market would
be large enough to support "efficient" production of ProductI
than ProductII. Hence, the United States export performance
of Product II should be better than for Product I.

It was assumed that the total market in units for the two
products was the same at a given income. If it is assumed
that the number of units of Product II sold were twice that of
Product I at the same income, the number of plants which
could support lowest cost production would be the same for
both products and the export performance should be similar.

Thus, one measure of scale-economies which might be
related to export performance is the number of plants in
the United States which can support minimum cost production.
This number takes into account the size of the market at
a given income and the location of the low-point on the cost
curve.

This measure is, of course, not perfect. If the rates

of decline of the cost curves are different, the measure may give a larger number of plants for the item with the lower slope, as some plants may be operating below the optimum point without too much penalty. However, for such products, a foreigner may initiate production earlier, as his penalty is also lower. Hence, the number of plants in the United States reflects the low point and the slope of the cost curve, but the export data may also reflect these two characteristics.

This number is also not stable over the life-cycle of a product. In the early stages, there are often many producers, trying different specifications of the product. Many of these will soon fail, as a few producers attain volume and low costs. [20]

---

20. We find a good example of this "shake-out" in Rae, op. cit. On pp. 18-21 and 62, Rae says that there have been 1500 identifiable manufacturers of cars and trucks in the United States. The great majority had failed by World War I. The early cars offered a wide choice of features: steam-power, electric-power, gasoline-power, water-cooled, air-cooled, single-cylinder, multi-cylinder, etc. However, the trend was finally clear—multi-cylinder, 4-cycle, water-cooled (usually), gasoline-powered vehicles. Those who did not adapt to this trend failed.

Every other motor-vehicle in the world was a Model-T by 1920. The small competitors could not survive against Ford's low costs at these volumes.

The story of the electronics industry in Hall, op. cit., pp. 259-277, provides a similar example.

Hence, a stable number is reached only when some maturity is attained in the industry. With the possible exception of room air conditioners, all of the products in the sample have probably passed through the "shake-out" stage. If electric-toothbrushes had been included, for example, the number of establishments in the industry in 1963 would probably have been a very inaccurate measure of the possible scale-economies.

The measure may also be affected by the degree of competition and by differing price-elasticities. However, as the product progresses toward the "mature" stage, the price-elasticity for each individual firm becomes higher as product differentiation becomes more difficult. Due to the difficulty of getting theoretical production cost curves for individual products, the number of plants in the United States will be used as a measure of the scale-economies relative to the market size for the product.

Given a good measure of the number of plants producing a product in the United States, a more rapid rate of decline should be found in exports of those products which are produced by a large number of plants. The scale-economies should put a ceiling on the amplitude of the export curve, or the amount of exports of a given industry at a given time. Exports as a percentage of production should be higher, then, for products produced by only a few plants in the United States.

To test these hypotheses, a crude index of dispersion was calculated for each product, which should reflect the number of plants producing the product in the United States. The four-digit SIC industry containing each product was found. The number of establishments with 20 or more employees in the industry was multiplied by the ratio of the shipments of the individual product to that of the four-digit industry. [21]

The assumption was made that each four-digit industry was homogeneous and that the number of plants could be assigned proportionally to the output of each product. This assumption was felt to be poor for two cases, recreational watercraft and room air conditioners. Recreational watercraft production is included in SIC 3732, Boat Building and Repairing. No doubt, boat repairing is very different from boat building and accounts for the large number of establishments. Moreover, it seems likely that the technologies for different types of boat building are very different. Room air conditioners are included in SIC 3585, Refrigerators,

---

21. Data from the Department of Commerce Industry Reports, 1963 Census of Manufactures.

Refrigeration Machinery, except Household, and Complete
Air Conditioning Units. Probably the construction of room
air conditioners is more similar to that of household refrigerators and freezers than to that of commercial refrigeration
equipment. Hence, an adjustment was made to the index
of dispersion for air conditioners to account for this assumption. Table III-24 gives the index of dispersion for each of
the products for which sufficient data were available. [22]

Figures III-8 and III-9 show the index of dispersion
plotted against the ratio of 1962-1963 average exports to
1952-1953 average exports for each of the products and the
index plotted against 1962-1963 average exports as a percentage of 1963 factory shipments.

---

22. Another problem occurs with products where several
    stages of manufacture exist and the returns-to-scale
    are very different. For example, the returns-to-scale
    for compressors seem much greater than for the assembly
    of refrigerators. The index will probably reflect the lower-
    scale operation more heavily. If this is the final assembly
    operation, as it probably is in most cases, then the index
    will be the correct one for predicting exports of the final
    product. It will be noted that the exports of refrigerators
    are measured, not the exports of compressors which may,
    and probably do, behave very differently.

Table III-24

Index of Dispersion

Product	Index of Dispersion
OTB	8.7
MVC	2.2
STC	5.7*
SLP	2.3
AUT	54
RAN	52
FRE	2.7
WSR	2.1
DRR	6.1
TV	138
RAD	41.7
REC	14
ARC	5**
VAC	13
BOT	180***

*1958 data

**Unadjusted calculation gave "56". See text.

***Probably overstated. See text.

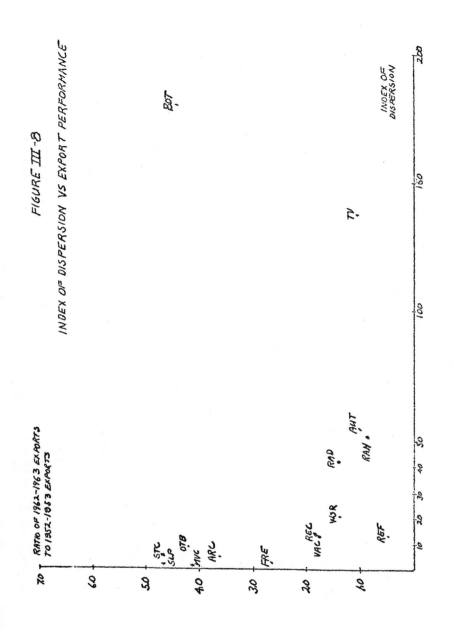

FIGURE III-8

INDEX OF DISPERSION VS EXPORT PERFORMANCE

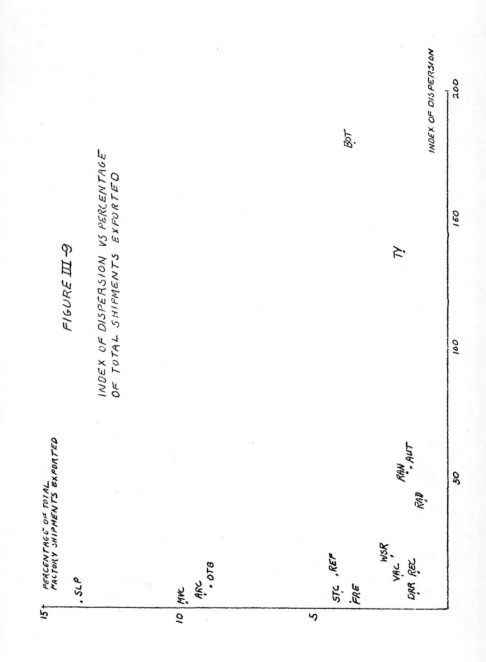

FIGURE III-9

INDEX OF DISPERSION VS PERCENTAGE
OF TOTAL SHIPMENTS EXPORTED

PERCENTAGE OF TOTAL
FACTORY SHIPMENTS EXPORTED

INDEX OF DISPERSION

Figure III-8 does indicate that there is a relation between
scale and export performance as predicted. It does appear
that the exports have performed better for products where the
index of dispersion is low.

Figure III-9 also seems to be in agreement with the model.
It appears that a certain degree of concentration is necessary
before exports amount to a large percentage of production.
This is not simply an oligopoly effect. Note the case of automobiles where the industry is probably oligopolistic. Exports
are small as a percentage of output. The number of companies
is small, but the number of plants is large.

Unfortunately, the number of products for which the index
of dispersion could be calculated was too small to allow for
a multiple correlation test with the index of dispersion and
elasticity as independent variables and United States export
performance as the dependent variable.

It appears, though, from the limited sample, that the
data are in agreement with the hypotheses about changes in
exports and the percentage of output exported. A more
accurate measure of the number of plants producing each
product might make a very good predictor of United States
export performance.

168

TRANSPORTATION AND TARIFFS

In order to test the prediction that transportation and tariffs affect the United States export position by offering more protection to the foreigner, a value per unit weight index was calculated and the tariffs for the United Kingdom, the European Economic Community, and Canada were collected for each product. Tables III-25 and III-26 give the results of these calculations.

In order to test the effect of transportation costs on United States exports, it was assumed that the ranking of value per unit weight and the ranking of shipping costs per unit value would be exactly opposite. The next step was to take those items which had an index of dispersion less than 25 and to rank correlate the exports as a percentage of shipments with the value per unit weight. The model would predict that, given a sufficient degree of concentration such that exports are possible, those products which have lower transportation costs, i. e. higher value per unit weight, would perform better as exports. Table III-27 gives the rankings and the Spearman's Coefficient of Rank Correlation. The percentage of exports to shipments appears to be positively correlated with the value per unit weight. The coefficient

Table III-25

Value Per Unit Weight[*]

Product	Value/Weight ($/lb)
OTB	3.9
MVC	16.7
STC	5.0
SLP	3.2
AUT	0.6
MIX	2.0
IR	2.4
REF	0.7
RAN	0.8
FRE	1.4
DWR	1.1
WSR	0.7
DRR	.5
TV	3.1
RAD	4-10[**]
REC	1.6
ARC	1.0
VAC	2.0
ECL	4.7
BOT	1.2

[*] The least expensive version was chosen from the Sears Roebuck Catalog, Fall and Winter 1965, and the ratio of space to shipping weight was calculated. Where export data was available by type, the value/weight was weighted by the exports of each type.

[**] The range of versions was too wide to arrive at a meaningful number.

Table III-26

Tariffs for E. E. C. , Canada, and U. K.

Product	E. E. C.	Canada	U. K.
OTB	18	0-22 1/2	17 1/2
MVC	16	0-9	40
STC	18	0-20	20-50
SLP	18	10-20	42. 5
AUT	29	17 1/2	30
MIX	19	20-22 1/2	15-17 1/2
IR	20	22 1/2	20
REF	13	20-22 1/2	15
RAN	n. a.	n. a.	n. a.
FRE	13	20-22 1/2	15
DWR	18	22 1/2	15
WSR	19	22 1/2	17 1/2
DRR	19	22 1/2	17 1/2
TV	22	20-22 1/2	20
RAD	22	20-22 1/2	20
REC	19	15-20	20
ARC	13	20-22 1/2	15
VAC	19	20-22 1/2	15-17 1/2
ECL	15	30	33 1/3
BOT	10 (avg)	0-25	10

Table III-27

Transportation Ranked Against Percentage of Shipments Exported

Product	Rank by Percentage of Shipments Exported	Rank by Value per Unit Weight
SLP	1	4
MVC	2	1
OTB	3	3
REF	4	6
STC	5	2
FRE	6	8
WSR	7	7
VAC	8	5
DRR	9.5	10
REC	9.5	6

Spearman's Coefficient of Rank Correlation = .706

of .706 is significant at the .05 level, but not at the .01
level. In order to test for cross-correlation with the
other variables, Spearman's Coefficients were calculated
for value per unitweight ranked with income-elasticity
of ownership and with saturation. No significant correlation
was found (See Table III-28). It appears, then, that, given
protection through scale-economies related to market
size, the transportation costs are significant in determining
the amount of exports which can be attained.

Table III-26 shows no apparent pattern in the duties
for a particular product. As the duties vary from country
to country, a conclusion as to the strength of the relationship
of tariffs to United States exports will have to wait for
an analysis of United States exports by country of destination.

CONCLUSIONS OF EMPIRICAL TEST

The empirical test presented in this chapter has demonstrated
a strong relationship between the income-nature of consumer
durables and the change in their export performance. Luxury
goods have performed better than discretionary goods, which
in turn have performed better than necessity goods. 80% of
the variance in the change in average exports for 1962-1963

Table III-23

Test of Cross-correlation of Value Per Unit Weight with
Elasticity and Saturation

Product	Rank by Value per Unit Weight	Rank by Income Elasticity	Rank by Saturation
SLP	4	1	9
MVC	1	2	8
OTB	3	4	10
REF	6	10	1
STC	2	6	4
FRE	8	7	6
WSR	7	9	2
VAC	5	8	3
DRR	10	3	7
REC	6	5	5

R_1 = Spearman's Rank Correlation Coefficient for value per
unit weight and income elasticity = .353

R_2 = Spearman's Rank Correlation Coefficient for value per
unit weight and saturation = -.180

from the average exports of 1952-1953 could be explained
by the income-elasticity of ownership. It was observed that
this better performance for highly income-elastic goods is
not due to a sharing in increasing world exports of these
products, but appears to be a comparative advantage
phenomenon. Moreover, for the consumer durables which
were studied, the United States does indeed seem to have a
price advantage in the higher-quality versions of the product.

In addition, differences in scale-economies do seem to
play a role in determining the differences in export performance. It appears that United States exports have performed
better for products where the scale-economies are large
relative to the market size. Moreover, large scale-economies
relative to market size appear to be a necessary, but not
sufficient condition for a large percentage of the United
States production of a given product to be exported.

Also, transportation costs do appear to provide protection to the foreign manufacturer. The United States
has done better exporting products for which the transportation
costs are low relative to the value of the item.

CHAPTER IV

A BASIS FOR POLICY

Chapter II proposed an hypothesis to explain United States export performance in consumer durables. According to this hypothesis, if everything else is held constant, the United States should perform better exporting consumer durables which appeal more to high-income groups than those which have a wider appeal. The hypothesis also predicted, again if everything else is equal, that the United States exports of products for which the optimal plant size is large relative to the total market size will perform better than those for which the size is small relative to the market. In addition, the model forecast that the United States would perform better exporting products for which transportation costs and duties are low.

Chapter III presented an empirical test of the ability of the hypothesis to explain trade patterns in consumer durables. Each of the variables which were considered in the hypothesis was correlated with performance measures of United States exports of consumer durables. In every case except duties, a strong correlation in the direction predicted was found. No significant difference was discovered in the average duties for the products. Hence, verification of this part of the hypothesis must await a study based on the destination of United States exports.

The consistency of the data with the proposed hypothesis lends considerable support to the conclusion that the model may be a useful tool for predicting United States export performance in consumer durables. Moreover, since the assumptions and the argument are applicable to many other product groups, the model may be useful for explaining or predicting some other trade patterns.

RELATION TO OTHER MODELS

The hypothesis developed in Chapter II is, of course, closely related to the explanations of trade patterns advanced by Vernon, Burenstam Linder, Hirsch, Hufbauer, Douglass, and Keesing, which were discussed in some detail in the first chapter. It might be useful to look at each of these hypotheses to see where they differ from our model and what they have in common with it.

The Trade Cycle Models

Burenstam Linder predicted that a country would be a potential exporter of products for which it has a "representative" demand. Vernon agreed with Burenstam Linder and concluded that the United States has a unique "representative" demand for high-income and labor-saving products. Vernon and Hirsch added dynamic elements to the hypothesis, concluding that the United States advantage declines over the product cycle.

Our model is similar to Burenstam Linder's and Vernon's hypotheses. We claim that the United States has the largest high-income market, and thus attains an advantage in high-income products.

If Vernon's labor saving products include only products which substitute a large amount of capital for a unit of labor, these products may also be considered to be high-income, in a sense. Since per capita income and wage rates are closely correlated, a country which has a high wage rate and thus can afford to substitute large amounts of capital for a man-hour saved can be considered to be a high-income country. Vernon probably did mean that the United States would have an advantage only in this type of labor-saving product. The United States probably would perform well for a longer period of time exporting fork-lift trucks than it would exporting screw-holding screw drivers. The first product substitutes a lot of capital for a unit of labor saved. The second is a simple tool which requires little capital per unit of labor saved. No doubt, efficient production for the latter item would start much sooner overseas because the market would be larger. It is of course a useless argument as to whether "high-income" or "labor-saving" is a better expression to describe such products. Many products may be easily described with both terms--household dishwashers, for example. The point is that if "labor-saving" is restricted to those items which require a lot of capital per unit of labor saved (which is probably the case for most new labor-saving products), then the descriptions are equivalent.[1]

Our export cycle is similar to Vernon's, and to Hirsch's if Hirsch's "new products" are restricted to "new, high-

---

1. For an interesting study of the effect of scarcity of labor on the development of labor-saving devices, see Habakkuk, H. J., American and British Technology in the Nineteenth Century; The Search for Labour-Saving Inventions, Cambridge University Press, Cambridge, 1962.

income products. " From our argument, it follows that the
United States would not have an advantage in all new products.
The example of stainless steel razor blades has already been
cited. Even such technically-advanced products as certain
bagasse boards were introduced in underdeveloped countries.
They were inexpensive substitutes for expensive lumber
and plastics.[2] Of course, there may be a tendency for the
majority of new products to be high-income products.

Our model is similar to Burenstam Linder's with
an elaboration of dynamic factors, similar to Vernon's if
the meaning of "labor-saving" is restricted, and similar
to Hirsch's if his "new products" must also be " high-
income. "

The Technological Gap Models

The technological gap hypotheses' emphasis on supply
factors is not adequate to explain the flows of international trade in

---

2. See Business Week, March 23, 1963, pp. 137-138.

consumer durables, although it is probably very useful for
certain other product groups. There is little difference in
the technological content of the United States imports and exports for most consumer durables.

The addition of an analysis of demand factors may add to
the ability of the technological gap hypotheses to explain trade
in synthetics studied by Hufbauer and to explain why the United
States gained a lead in innovation in the movie industry which
was studied by Douglass.

In the case of synthetics, the demand argument could
run as follows: Some synthetics appeal to a high-income market
exclusively. They are used for their special qualities and not
for cost savings. One might expect the United States to gain an
advantage in exporting such products. However, for certain
synthetics, Germany had a strong internal demand. With the
risk of being cut-off from sources of natural raw materials in
wartime, Germany was willing to accept high costs to have
alternative domestic sources of supply. The United States was
less dependent on foreign sources for many of its raw materials
and was presumably planning less for war. Hence, Germany
may have had a larger market for those synthetics which could
enable it to be more self-sufficient in war and was able to
become an exporter of such products.

In the case of the movie industry, each of the innovations mentioned by Douglass raised the cost of movies. The box office price was raised. Average unit costs certainly decline with volume in the movie industry, where the incremental cost of an additional print is low. The United States market was large enough to spread the increased fixed cost over a large number of prints and had a sufficiently high-income population to pay the increased ticket price. The United States was able to export prints at comparatively low prices (probably at slightly above incremental cost.[3]). Such an explanation is consistent with Vernon's, Burenstam Linder's and our models.

Labor Skill and Research and Development Content

Keesing found that labor skill and research and development content were useful as predictors of United States export performance. No doubt, a study of a broader sample of products than was included in our test would yield a close correlation between high-income products and their skilled labor and research and development content, at least at early stages in the product cycle.

---

3. Douglass, op. cit., p. 254.

However, Keesing's concentration on the supply side is
again insufficient to explain many of the patterns observed in
our sample of consumer durables. There is certainly no reason
to believe that larger-capacity refrigerators and freezers
have a greater research and development or skilled labor
content than do small ones. Similarly, there is no reason to
believe that room air conditioners have more of these two inputs
than do freezers, or freezers more than refrigerators. Probably
for consumer durables there is at the most only a weak correlation between the income-appeal of the product and its technological content.

No doubt, the supply of skilled labor and research and development capacity does act as a limiting factor on a country's export
ability. One would not expect some of the underdeveloped
countries to be able to export products requiring great quantities
of labor skill or of research and development. However, for a
broad range of countries, an analysis based on the supply of
these factors seems inadequate to explain the observed trade
patterns in certain goods. Certainly Israel has a large supply of
relatively cheap scientists and engineers and could export
technically advanced products. Surely Germany could, viewed

_____

4. See Hirsch, op. cit.

from the supply side, produce large refrigerators or quality electric mixers as cheaply as could the United States. Keesing's model may, though, be very useful as a predictive device in certain industries which are very skill and technology oriented. No doubt, in many cases an analysis of both the demand and supply sides is necessary. The case of consumer durables does illustrate the necessity of including the demand side for certain products.

Heckscher-Ohlin and Leontief

It is interesting to note that our model is consistent with Leontief's findings. New, high-income products are probably more labor-intensive during the period when the United States is a net exporter than they are later in the export cycle when the United States has lost its export advantage. Max Hall mentions the lower capital intensity of new products:

> "When new products are born, the technology of production does not usually demand large capital investment. It is only later, when the technology settles down and when specialized machinery and specialized plant layouts come into use, that the need for a large capital investment may develop."[5]

---

5. Hall, (ed.), op. cit., p. 259.

Demand vs. Supply Analysis

We would certainly not suggest that our model is adequate to explain all trade flows in manufactures. What we have done, though, is to demonstrate the influence of demand factors on trade patterns in certain products. The patterns which were explained in the test in Chapter III could not be explained by supply factors alone.

There is no question that supply factors are also relevant to trade patterns in a large number of goods. Obviously, if the product is "resource-oriented," i. e. depends to a great extent on proximity to inputs which are not available in many countries, then location of these inputs is important in determining trade patterns. These inputs may be of particular labor skills (diamond cutters, for example) or of particular raw materials for which bulk, duties, or perishability make transportation to another site for processing expensive (perhaps certain processed fish foods like canned anchovies fit this pattern). However, for a wide range of manufactured goods, the inputs consist primarily of such items as ferrous metals which are available at not too different costs in all the developed countries and of not very advanced technical and production skills which are not scarce in all the industrial world.

Only an analysis of the demand side can adequately explain the
very different and constantly shifting trade patterns in these
products which appear to have similar manufacturing inputs.

EXPORTS, IMPORTS, AND THE BUSINESSMAN

The hypothesis which was developed to explain trade patterns
in consumer durables can be used as a tool to help the businessman
to select which of his products have a good export potential
and to help him to guess in advance which of his products will
be threated by import competition.

Exports

The American who is interested in export markets for his
products can identify certain characteristics which may indicate
that they could be exported successfully. Those products for
which the United States manufacturer has gained scale-economies
which would not be available to a foreigner producing for his
own market may be potentially successful exports.   If the
transportation and duty costs are not sufficiently high to make
up for the disadvantage suffered by the foreigner because of the
small size of his market, the product will probably be a good

bet for export.

Those products for which the United States market is the only one large enough for scale-economies to be reached are usually products which appeal much more strongly to high-income consumers (Vernon's hypothesis, which we have not tested, would include new products which replace labor with capital). The relative appeal of products to different income groups can usually be estimated by referring to the many studies of household expenditure and ownership patterns in the United States. Although we have indicated that foreign preferences tend to be similar to United States consumption patterns for consumer durables, the businessman can often verify the similarity for a particular product by reference to one of the many foreign market studies. [6]

---

6. For example, a recent German study predicted rapid growth next in dishwashers and freezers, and, in the future, in dryers, garbage disposals, and air conditioners. There is probably a good opportunity for United States exports of the latter products until the German market is large enough to support large-scale production. See Zerralen, Kurt, "Das Aktuelle Marktbild fuer Haushalt-Grossgeraete," in NEFF-WERKE, Der Haushalt Grossgeraete-Markt von Morgen, Econ-Verlag, Duesseldorf, 1965.

Having identified potential export products in this way, the businessman must decide where his foreign markets lie. The advanced, industrial countries offer the largest market for high-income products. However, high-income segments of less-developed countries may also offer profitable export opportunities.

The exporter can, according to the hypothesis of this study, expect to lose his markets in the developed countries to local production after a period. When the markets have become large enough, local production, with cheaper wage rates and the savings of transportation and duty costs, will displace American exports. For a while, the American may be able to hold onto his markets in less-developed countries.

As markets in the other developed countries grow, their exports will become more competitive in the third markets and will displace United States exports.

The exporter must continually shift his emphasis to higher-income products to replace those exports which have been displaced by foreign manufacture. He must plan for a "roll-over" in his product line. The exporter who is ready with dishwashers when foreign competition for clothes washers becomes too great is the one who will profit.

The exporter can maintain his competitiveness longer, however, by making use of the knowledge that the United States is more likely to be competitive in higher-quality versions[7.] of a product. By carefully matching the type of product which he promotes for export to the characteristics of the market and to the type of competition he expects, the exporter may be able to extend the period during which he is competitive.

To analyze the type of product which should be offered, it is useful to look at three phases in the cycle during which the United States is competitive: Phase I, when the United States is the only major producer, Phase II, when local production has started in the other advanced countries, and Phase III, when the other advanced countries have begun to export to the less-developed countries.

During Phase I. the United States has a monopoly. It can sell any version of the product, and will probably offer simply that version which is most in demand in the United States.

---

7. The term as used here, as in Chapter II refers to variations on the product which cause it to appeal to higher-income consumers, such as larger capacity, more automatic features, etc.

Exports may be somewhat larger, however, if a simple version
is offered.

In Phase II, the other advanced countries will probably
have begun to produce a simpler version of the product than
is currently being manufactured in the United States. The
United States can only compete in the advanced countries with
more complex versions which either are not produced at all
locally or are produced only in small volume. --large refrigerators, automatic washing machines, etc. In the less-developed
areas, the United States will still have a monopoly on high-
quality versions, but it should also offer simpler versions if
they can be produced as adaptations of the model made for the
United States market. Otherwise, exports of the simpler
versions produced in the other developed countries will appear
particularly attractive to the lower-income consumer in these
countries. [8]

---

8. An example of a company which successfully followed such
a policy in Peru for ranges is mentioned in United States
Department of Commerce, Major Household Appliances,
pp. 42-45. Although American ranges were supposedly
of better design and had more gadgets, the European
models held most of the market because of their lower prices.
One American company was, however, successfully marketing
a stripped-down version of the American product. It is
interesting to note that American manufacturers dominated
the market for freezers, a higher-income product.

In Phase III, simpler versions of the product are produced more cheaply in other advanced countries and will capture a large part of the market in the less-developed countries. The United States may still be competitive in higher-income variations of the product, however.

Of course, there may be two more phases in the complete cycle. The less-developed countries may become producers for their own market and, finally, they may become exporters. However, few products seem to have moved into this last stage. Perhaps textiles and small transistor radios may be cited as examples of products in this latter phase.

Figure IV-1 summarizes the competitiveness of United States exports of various qualities of a product in the three phases which have been discussed.

Imports

The hypothesis also predicts that the United States manufacturer will be threatened by imports if foreign markets are sufficiently large that scale-economies can be reached and if the United States manufacturer is not protected by sufficient

Figure IV-1

Competitiveness of Various Qualities of

a Product

Phase	Quality Competitive in	
	Other Advanced Countries	Less-Developed Countries
I. New, high-income product; only major production in U.S.	All	All
II. Other advanced countries have begun production	High-quality	All
III. Other advanced countries have begun to export	Perhaps very high-quality	High-quality

transportation and duty costs. [9.] These first imports will, according to the hypothesis, come from other advanced countries and they will usually be lower-quality versions of the product then being produced in the United States. The United States manufacturer may be able to hold a large segment of the market through the introduction of features which cause the product to have more appeal to the higher-income American consumer. Larger, higher-powered cars, for example, have certainly helped the American automobile manufacturers to maintain a large share of the United States market in the face of import competition. In some cases, the American manufacturer may have to give up supplying from American plants a segment of the market which is interested primarily in price.

Income-Appeal

When the businessman is looking at the income-appeal of

---

9. An example of the effect of scale economies on the competitive position of the American manufacturer is given by the announcement of the intention of Spanish companies to enter the American automobile parts market with items characterized by small production-runs in the United States. The companies are an "outgrowth of the booming Spanish automotive production." They have already begun to supply Common Market countries and are beginning a push in Latin America. See Jones, Brendan, "Spain to Sell Auto Parts in U. S. A.," New York Times, February 14, 1966, p. 43.

his products, he must be careful to distinguish what may be a temporary phenomenon and what is the long-run appeal of the product. The fact that new products tend to have an initial appeal to a high-income market may lead to an erroneous classification. An analysis of the needs which are met by the product, the availability of substitutes, and the cost of the product when mass-production is introduced should lead to appropriate adjustments to the estimates. For example, the portable transistor radio was high-priced and appealed to high-income consumers as a kind of toy initially. However, the product fulfilled such basic universal needs for which no good substitute was available (portable source of communication and entertainment, free of the need for a power supply, with long-distance reception, etc.), and the price fell so much as mass-production began that it soon appealed widely to low-income groups. Markets in less-developed countries were quickly very large and the product moved through the trade cycle very rapidly. The time period was very short from when the United States was an exporter of a then high-income product to when less-developed countries were producing and exporting small transistor radios.

In contrast, the electric-toothbrush will probably not appeal to such a wide range of consumers. Its function can easily be performed by a conventional toothbrush. It may do the job slightly better, but its additional cost and its dependence on a nearby source of power will probably mean that it will go through a rather slow trade cycle, with the United States having an initial advantage, and then after a period, European or Japanese production becoming competitive.

Conclusion

These examples show that it is necessary and possible to predict the income-appeal of products in the future. From this income-appeal, export opportunities and import competition may be forecast for many products.

Above all, it is important to recognize that patterns of trade are constantly changing and that the successful business-man must be able to predict and respond quickly to the opportunities and threats which are posed by international trade. As transportation becomes more rapid and cheaper, as communications grow more efficient, and as barriers to trade come down, not only may the rate of change in trade patterns be increasing, but the size of the opportunities and the magnitude of the threats are almost certain to grow.

APPENDIX

CHARACTERISTICS OF REGRESSIONS
FOR INCOME-ELASTICITY OF OWNERSHIP
FOR CONSUMER DURABLES

197

TVNO

CORRELATION COEFFICIENT FOR EACH VARIABLE -SQUARED
0.98600930

ORIGINAL MATRIX
0.10667068E 01
0.28707800E 00

INVERSE MATRIX
0.93746473E 00

COEFFICIENTS
0.26912550E 00
CONSTANT TERM   0.30044551E 01

TOTAL SUM OF SQUARES   0.78197800E-01
SUM OF SQUARES REMOVED BY REGRESSION   0.77260010E-01
RESIDUAL SUM OF SQUARES   0.93779000E-03

STANDARD ERROR OF ESTIMATE   0.12501933E-01
MULTIPLE CORRELATION COEFFICIENT   0.99297971E 00

F,K,N-K-1
0.49431116E 03,   1,   6

FOR EACH COEFFICIENT

STANDARD ERROR   T
0.12104717E-01   0.22233110E 02

198

RADNO   CORRELATION COEFFICIENT FOR EACH VARIABLE -SQUARED
                              0.92579784

ORIGINAL MATRIX
0.10667068E 01
0.45518480E 00

INVERSE MATRIX
0.93746473E 00

COEFFICIENTS
0.42671970E 00
CONSTANT TERM   0.26083248E 01

TOTAL SUM OF SQUARES   0.20742930E 00
SUM OF SQUARES REMOVED BY REGRESSION   0.19423632E 00
RESIDUAL SUM OF SQUARES   0.13192980E-01

STANDARD ERROR OF ESTIMATE   0.46891684E-01
MULTIPLE CORRELATION COEFFICIENT   0.96218362E 00

F,K,N-K-1
0.88336215E 02,   1,   6

FOR EACH COEFFICIENT

STANDARD ERROR   T
0.45401824E-01   0.93987347E 01

AUTO

CORRELATION COEFFICIENT FOR EACH VARIABLE —SQUARED
0.87522785

ORIGINAL MATRIX
0.10667068E 01
0.48757950E 00

INVERSE MATRIX
0.93746473E 00

COEFFICIENTS
0.45708858E 00
CONSTANT TERM   0.21362579E 01

TOTAL SUM OF SQUARES   0.24955850E 00
SUM OF SQUARES REMOVED BY REGRESSION   0.22286702E 00
RESIDUAL SUM OF SQUARES   0.26691480E-01

STANDARD ERROR OF ESTIMATE   0.66697676E-01
MULTIPLE CORRELATION COEFFICIENT   0.93553161E 00

F,K,N-K-1
0.50098463E 02,   1,   6

FOR EACH COEFFICIENT

STANDARD ERROR   T
0.64578532E-01   0.70780268E 01

AUTNO

CORRELATION COEFFICIENT FOR EACH VARIABLE -SQUARED
0.98001457

ORIGINAL MATRIX
0.10667068E 01
0.66181160E 00

INVERSE MATRIX
0.93746473E 00

COEFFICIENTS
0.62042503E 00
CONSTANT TERM   0.16129099E 01

TOTAL SUM OF SQUARES   0.41775690E 00
SUM OF SQUARES REMOVED BY REGRESSION   0.41060448E 00
RESIDUAL SUM OF SQUARES   0.71524200E-02

STANDARD ERROR OF ESTIMATE   0.34526367E-01
MULTIPLE CORRELATION COEFFICIENT   0.98996237E 00

F,K,N-K-1
0.34444662E 03,   1,   6

FOR EACH COEFFICIENT

STANDARD ERROR   T
0.33429382E-01   0.18559273E 02

REC

CORRELATION COEFFICIENT FOR EACH VARIABLE —SQUARED
0.95252586

ORIGINAL MATRIX
0.10667068E 01
0.68497430E 00

INVERSE MATRIX
0.93746473E 00

COEFFICIENTS
0.64213925E 00
CONSTANT TERM   0.12371908E 01

TOTAL SUM OF SQUARES   0.45850850E 00
SUM OF SQUARES REMOVED BY REGRESSION   0.43984888E 00
RESIDUAL SUM OF SQUARES   0.18659620E-01

STANDARD ERROR OF ESTIMATE   0.55766806E-01
MULTIPLE CORRELATION COEFFICIENT   0.97597179E 00

F,K,N-K-1
0.14143339E 03,   1,   6

FOR EACH COEFFICIENT

STANDARD ERROR   T
0.53994962E-01   0.11892577E 02

TV

CORRELATION COEFFICIENT FOR EACH VARIABLE -SQUARED

0.87167074

ORIGINAL MATRIX
0.10667068E 01
0.15671330E 00

INVERSE MATRIX
0.93746473E 00

COEFFICIENTS
0.14691319E 00
CONSTANT TERM   0.33996469E 01

TOTAL SUM OF SQUARES   0.25866800E-01
SUM OF SQUARES REMOVED BY REGRESSION   0.23023251E-01
RESIDUAL SUM OF SQUARES   0.28435490E-02

STANDARD ERROR OF ESTIMATE   0.21769815E-01
MULTIPLE CORRELATION COEFFICIENT   0.93367436E 00

F,K,N-K-1   0.48579963E 02,   1,   6

FOR EACH COEFFICIENT

STANDARD ERROR   T
0.21078136E-01   0.69699327E 01

MIX

CORRELATION COEFFICIENT FOR EACH VARIABLE -SQUARED

0.93855401

ORIGINAL MATRIX
0.10667068E 01
0.40753800E 00

INVERSE MATRIX
0.93746473E 00

COEFFICIENTS
0.38205250E 00
CONSTANT TERM   0.23691678E 01

TOTAL SUM OF SQUARES   0.16435730E 00
SUM OF SQUARES REMOVED BY REGRESSION   0.15570091E 00
RESIDUAL SUM OF SQUARES   0.86563900E-02

STANDARD ERROR OF ESTIMATE   0.37983308E-01
MULTIPLE CORRELATION COEFFICIENT   0.96878989E 00

F,K,N-K-1
        0.10792091E 03,   1,   6

FOR EACH COEFFICIENT

STANDARD ERROR   T
0.36776488E-01   0.10388499E 02

REF

CORRELATION COEFFICIENT FOR EACH VARIABLE -SQUARED
0.75560745

ORIGINAL MATRIX
0.10667068E 01
0.34380800E-01

INVERSE MATRIX
0.93746473E 00

COEFFICIENTS
0.32230787E-01
CONSTANT TERM   0.38706493E 01

TOTAL SUM OF SQUARES   0.13998000E-02
SUM OF SQUARES REMOVED BY REGRESSION   0.11081202E-02
RESIDUAL SUM OF SQUARES   0.29167980E-03

STANDARD ERROR OF ESTIMATE   0.69723239E-02
MULTIPLE CORRELATION COEFFICIENT   0.86999929E 00

F,K,N-K-1
0.22794589E 02,   1,   6

FOR EACH COEFFICIENT

STANDARD ERROR   T
0.67507966E-02   0.47743680E 01

RAN

CORRELATION COEFFICIENT FOR EACH VARIABLE -SQUARED
0.65545143

ORIGINAL MATRIX
0.10667068E 01
0.21789000E-01

INVERSE MATRIX
0.93746473E 00

COEFFICIENTS
0.20426419E-01
CONSTANT TERM   0.39177673E 01

TOTAL SUM OF SQUARES   0.62970000E-03
SUM OF SQUARES REMOVED BY REGRESSION   0.44507124E-03
RESIDUAL SUM OF SQUARES   0.18462876E-03

STANDARD ERROR OF ESTIMATE   0.55472029E-02
MULTIPLE CORRELATION COEFFICIENT   0.81113008E 00

F,K,N-K-1
          0.14463767E 02,   1,   6

FOR EACH COEFFICIENT

STANDARD ERROR   T
0.53709551E-02   0.38031260E 01

IR

CORRELATION COEFFICIENT FOR EACH VARIABLE -SQUARED
0.86736175

ORIGINAL MATRIX
0.10667068E 01
0.44828700E-01

INVERSE MATRIX
0.93746473E 00

COEFFICIENTS
0.42025325E-01
CONSTANT TERM   0.38276745E 01

TOTAL SUM OF SQUARES   0.21217000E-0?
SUM OF SQUARES REMOVED BY REGRESSION   0.18839407E-02
RESIDUAL SUM OF SQUARES   0.23775930E-C3

STANDARD ERROR OF ESTIMATE   0.62949623E-02
MULTIPLE CORRELATION COEFFICIENT   0.93234246E 00

F,K,N-K-1
0.47542385E 02,   1,   6

FOR EACH COEFFICIENT

STANDARD ERROR   T
0.60949564E-02   0.68950985E 01

BOT

CORRELATION COEFFICIENT FOR EACH VARIABLE -SQUARED
0.92690699

ORIGINAL MATRIX
0.10667068E 01
0.87806517E 00

INVERSE MATRIX
0.93746473E 00

COEFFICIENTS
0.82315513E 00
CONSTANT TERM   -0.36499636E 00

TOTAL SUM OF SQUARES   0.77109355E 00
SUM OF SQUARES REMOVED BY REGRESSION   0.72278385E 00
RESIDUAL SUM OF SQUARES   0.48309700E-01

STANDARD ERROR OF ESTIMATE   0.89730801E-01
MULTIPLE CORRELATION COEFFICIENT   0.96276025E 00

F,K,N-K-1
      0.89768786E 02,   1,   6

FOR EACH COEFFICIENT

STANDARD ERROR   T
0.86879840E-01   0.94746391E 01

ECL

CORRELATION COEFFICIENT FOR EACH VARIABLE -SQUARED
0.87162730

ORIGINAL MATRIX
0.10667068E 01
0.22785130E 00

INVERSE MATRIX
0.93746473E 00

COEFFICIENTS
0.21360256E 00
CONSTANT TERM   0.30596588E 01

TOTAL SUM OF SQUARES   0.54687000E-01
SUM OF SQUARES REMOVED BY REGRESSION   0.48669621E-01
RESIDUAL SUM OF SQUARES   0.60173790E-02

STANDARD ERROR OF ESTIMATE   0.31668541E-01
MULTIPLE CORRELATION COEFFICIENT   0.93361024E 00

F,K,N-K-1
0.48529057E 02,   1,   6

FOR EACH COEFFICIENT

STANDARD ERROR   T
0.30662356E-01   0.69662801E 01

SLP

CORRELATION COEFFICIENT FOR EACH VARIABLE —SQUARED
0.98217413

ORIGINAL MATRIX
0.10667068E 01
0.16277123E 01

INVERSE MATRIX
0.93746473E 00

COEFFICIENTS
0.15259229E 01
CONSTANT TERM   -0.29439231E 01

TOTAL SUM OF SQUARES   0.25223027E 01
SUM OF SQUARES REMOVED BY REGRESSION   0.24837635E 01
RESIDUAL SUM OF SQUARES   0.38539200E-01

STANDARD ERROR OF ESTIMATE   0.80144869E-01
MULTIPLE CORRELATION COEFFICIENT   0.99104696E 00

F,K,N-K-1
0.38668631E 03,   1,   6

FOR EACH COEFFICIENT

STANDARD ERROR   T
0.77598476E-01   0.19664341E 02

MVP

CORRELATION COEFFICIENT FOR EACH VARIABLE -SQUARED
0.90275770

ORIGINAL MATRIX
0.10667068E 01
0.14979966E 01

INVERSE MATRIX
0.93746473E 00

COEFFICIENTS
0.14043190E 01
CONSTANT TERM   -0.24500056E 01

TOTAL SUM OF SQUARES   0.22949502E 01
SUM OF SQUARES REMOVED BY REGRESSION   0.21036651E 01
RESIDUAL SUM OF SQUARES   0.19128510E 00

STANDARD ERROR OF ESTIMATE   0.17855209E 00
MULTIPLE CORRELATION COEFFICIENT   0.95013569E 00

F,K,N-K-1
0.65985226E 02,   1,   6

FOR EACH COEFFICIENT

STANDARD ERROR   T
0.17287907E 00   0.81231291E 01

OTB

CORRELATION COEFFICIENT FOR EACH VARIABLE -SQUARED
0.84271859

ORIGINAL MATRIX
0.10667068E 01
0.94505735E 00

INVERSE MATRIX
0.93746473E 00

COEFFICIENTS
0.88595793E 00
CONSTANT TERM   -0.49651509E 00

TOTAL SUM OF SQUARES   0.96774560E 00
SUM OF SQUARES REMOVED BY REGRESSION   0.83728105E 00
RESIDUAL SUM OF SQUARES   0.13046455E 00

STANDARD ERROR OF ESTIMATE   0.14745878E 00
MULTIPLE CORRELATION COEFFICIENT   0.91799691E 00

F,K,N-K-1
       0.38506141E 02,   1,   6

FOR EACH COEFFICIENT

STANDARD ERROR   T
0.14277366E 00   0.62053318E 01

212

VAC   CORRELATION COEFFICIENT FOR EACH VARIABLE -SQUARED
0.91037968

ORIGINAL MATRIX
0.10667068E 01
0.36443030E 00

INVERSE MATRIX
0.93746473E 00

COEFFICIENTS
0.34164055E 00
CONSTANT TERM   0.25626784E 01

TOTAL SUM OF SQUARES   0.13486010E 00
SUM OF SQUARES REMOVED BY REGRESSION   0.12450417E 00
RESIDUAL SUM OF SQUARES   0.10355930E-01

STANDARD ERROR OF ESTIMATE   0.41545016E-01
MULTIPLE CORRELATION COEFFICIENT   0.95415484E 00

F,K,N-K-1
0.72135001E 02,   1,   6

FOR EACH COEFFICIENT

STANDARD ERROR   T
0.40225032E-01   0.84932325E 01

ARC

CORRELATION COEFFICIENT FOR EACH VARIABLE -SQUARED
0.95215100

ORIGINAL MATRIX
0.10667068E 01
0.86162629E 00

INVERSE MATRIX
0.93746473E 00

COEFFICIENTS
0.80774426E 00
CONSTANT TERM   -0.73569481E-01

TOTAL SUM OF SQUARES   0.72573873E 00
SUM OF SQUARES REMOVED BY REGRESSION   0.69597369E 00
RESIDUAL SUM OF SQUARES   0.29765040E-01

STANDARD ERROR OF ESTIMATE   0.70433231E-01
MULTIPLE CORRELATION COEFFICIENT   0.97578225E 00

F,K,N-K-1
0.14029352E 03,   1,   6

FOR EACH COEFFICIENT

STANDARD ERROR   T
0.68195400E-01   0.11844556E 02

DRR

CORRELATION COEFFICIENT FOR EACH VARIABLE -SQUARED
0.95296399

ORIGINAL MATRIX
0.10667068E 01
0.13317747E 01

INVERSE MATRIX
0.93746473E 00

COEFFICIENTS
0.12484918E 01
CONSTANT TERM   -0.15627208E 01

TOTAL SUM OF SQUARES   0.17325607E 01
SUM OF SQUARES REMOVED BY REGRESSION   0.16627098E 01
RESIDUAL SUM OF SQUARES   0.69850900E-01

STANDARD ERROR OF ESTIMATE   0.10789725E 00
MULTIPLE CORRELATION COEFFICIENT   0.97619875E 00

F,K,N-K-1
0.14282219E 03,   1,   6

FOR EACH COEFFICIENT

STANDARD ERROR   T
0.10446910E 00   0.11950824E 02

WSR

CORRELATION COEFFICIENT FOR EACH VARIABLE —SQUARED
0.77897666

ORIGINAL MATRIX
0.10667068E 01
0.16702650E 00

INVERSE MATRIX
0.93746473E 00

COEFFICIENTS
0.15658145E 00
CONSTANT TERM   0.32751515E 01

TOTAL SUM OF SQUARES   0.32268000E-01
SUM OF SQUARES REMOVED BY REGRESSION 0.26153252E-01
RESIDUAL SUM OF SQUARES   0.61147480E-02

STANDARD ERROR OF ESTIMATE   0.31923732E-01
MULTIPLE CORRELATION COEFFICIENT .   0.88256334E 00

F,K,N-K-1
0.25662466E 02,   1,   6

FOR EACH COEFFICIENT

                    T
STANDARD ERROR
0.30909439E-01   0.50658134E 01

DWR

CORRELATION COEFFICIENT FOR EACH VARIABLE -SQUARED
0.93120680

ORIGINAL MATRIX
0.10667068E 01
0.22529573E 01

INVERSE MATRIX
0.93746473E 00

COEFFICIENTS
0.21120680E 01
CONSTANT TERM   -0.55871864E 01

TOTAL SUM OF SQUARES   0.50565624E 01
SUM OF SQUARES REMOVED BY REGRESSION   0.47583990E 01
RESIDUAL SUM OF SQUARES   0.29816340E 00

STANDARD ERROR OF ESTIMATE   0.22292129E 00
MULTIPLE CORRELATION COEFFICIENT   0.96499055E 00

F,K,N-K-1
0.95754187E 02,   1,   6

FOR EACH COEFFICIENT

STANDARD ERROR   T
0.21583855E 00   0.97854067E 01

FRE

CORRELATION COEFFICIENT FOR EACH VARIABLE -SQUARED
0.96339527

ORIGINAL MATRIX
0.10667068E 01
0.49396438E 00

INVERSE MATRIX
0.93746473E 00

COEFFICIENTS
0.46307418E 00
CONSTANT TERM   0.15316779E 01

TOTAL SUM OF SQUARES   0.23615050E 00
SUM OF SQUARES REMOVED BY REGRESSION   0.22874215E 00
RESIDUAL SUM OF SQUARES   0.74083500E-02

STANDARD ERROR OF ESTIMATE   0.35138654E-01
MULTIPLE CORRELATION COEFFICIENT   0.98152949E 00

F,K,N-K-1
0.18525757E 03,   1,   6

FOR EACH COEFFICIENT

STANDARD ERROR   T
0.34022215E-01   0.13610936E 02

RECNO   CORRELATION COEFFICIENT FOR EACH VARIABLE -SQUARED
                        0.96157261

ORIGINAL MATRIX
   0.10667068E 01
   0.77810540E 00

INVERSE MATRIX
   0.93746473E 00

COEFFICIENTS
   0.72944637E 00
   CONSTANT TERM   0.96422500E 00

TOTAL SUM OF SQUARES   0.58691990E 00
SUM OF SQUARES REMOVED BY REGRESSION   0.56758616E 00
RESIDUAL SUM OF SQUARES   0.19333740E-01

STANDARD ERROR OF ESTIMATE   0.56765218E-01
MULTIPLE CORRELATION COEFFICIENT   0.98059615E 00

F,K,N-K-1
   0.17614372E 03,   1,   6

FOR EACH COEFFICIENT

STANDARD ERROR   T
   0.54961652E-01   0.13271915E 02

RAD

CORRELATION COEFFICIENT FOR EACH VARIABLE -SQUARED
0.94171045

ORIGINAL MATRIX
0.10667068E 01
0.97305000E-01

INVERSE MATRIX
0.93746473E 00

COEFFICIENTS
0.91220006E-01
CONSTANT TERM   0.36176300E 01

TOTAL SUM OF SQUARES   0.93390000E-02
SUM OF SQUARES REMOVED BY REGRESSION   0.88761627E-02
RESIDUAL SUM OF SQUARES   0.46283730E-03

STANDARD ERROR OF ESTIMATE   0.87829124E-02
MULTIPLE CORRELATION COEFFICIENT   0.97065980E 00

F,K,N-K-1
0.11506630E 03,   1,   6

FOR EACH COEFFICIENT

STANDARD ERROR   T
0.85038584E-02   0.10726896E 02

STC   CORRELATION COEFFICIENT FOR EACH VARIABLE -SQUARED
0.92159491

ORIGINAL MATRIX
0.10667068E 01
0.59531810E 00

INVERSE MATRIX
0.93746473E 00

COEFFICIENTS
0.55808972E 00
CONSTANT TERM   0.16805501E 01

TOTAL SUM OF SQUARES   0.35617360E 00
SUM OF SQUARES REMOVED BY REGRESSION   0.33224091E 00
RESIDUAL SUM OF SQUARES   0.23932690E-01

STANDARD ERROR OF ESTIMATE   0.63156802E-01
MULTIPLE CORRELATION COEFFICIENT   0.96000371E 00

F,K,N-K-1
0.83293832E 02,   1,   6

FOR EACH COEFFICIENT

STANDARD ERROR   T
0.61150160E-01   0.91265455E 01

MVC

CORRELATION COEFFICIENT FOR EACH VARIABLE -SQUARED

0.92533625

ORIGINAL MATRIX
0.10667068E 01
0.15808480E 01

INVERSE MATRIX
0.93746473E 00

COEFFICIENTS
0.14819892E 01
CONSTANT TERM   -0.26659920E 01

TOTAL SUM OF SQUARES   0.25029841E 01
SUM OF SQUARES REMOVED BY REGRESSION   0.23427997E 01
RESIDUAL SUM OF SQUARES   0.16018440E 00

STANDARD ERROR OF ESTIMATE   0.16339339E 00
MULTIPLE CORRELATION COEFFICIENT   0.96194407E 00

F,K,N-K-1
         0.87753852E 02,   1,   6

FOR EACH COEFFICIENT

STANDARD ERROR   T
0.15820199E 00   0.93677026E 01

MULTINATIONAL CORPORATIONS:
Operations and Finance

An Arno Press Collection

Aggarwal, Raj Kumar. **The Management of Foreign Exchange** (Doctoral Dissertation, Kent State University, 1975). Revised edition. 1980

Ahrari, Mohammed E. **The Dynamics of Oil Diplomacy** (Doctoral Dissertation, Southern Illinois University, 1976). 1980

Atkins, Edwin F[arnsworth]. **Sixty Years in Cuba.** 1926

Ayarslan, Solmaz D. **A Dynamic Stochastic Model for Current Asset and Liability Management of a Multinational Corporation** (Doctoral Dissertation, New York University, 1976). 1980

Bassiry, Reza. **Power vs. Profit** (Doctoral Dissertation, The State University of New York at Binghamton, 1977). 1980

Bodinat, Henri de. **Influence in the Multinational Corporation** (Doctoral Dissertation, Harvard University, 1975). 1980

Burgess, Eugene W., and Frederick H. Harbison. **Casa Grace in Peru.** 1954

Chandler, Alfred D., Jr., compiler and editor. **Giant Enterprise.** 1964

Cleveland, Harlan, Gerard J. Mangone, and John Clarke Adams. **The Overseas Americans.** 1960

Daniel, James, editor. **Private Investment.** 1958

Dubin, Michael. **Foreign Acquisitions and the Spread of the Multinational Firm** (Doctoral Dissertation, Harvard University, 1976). 1980

Finnie, David H. **Desert Enterprise.** 1958

Harrington, Fred Harvey. **God, Mammon, and the Japanese.** 1944

Heller, Kenneth Howard. **The Impact of U.S. Income Taxation on the Financing and Earnings Remittance Decisions of U.S.-Based Multinational Firms with Controlled Foreign Corporations** (Doctoral Dissertation, The University of Texas at Austin, 1977). 1980

Jadwani, Hassanand T. **Some Aspects of the Multinational Corporations' Exposure to the Exchange Rate Risk** (Doctoral Dissertation, Harvard University, 1971). 1980

Jeannet, Jean-Pierre. **Transfer of Technology within Multinational Corporations** (Doctoral Dissertation, The University of Massachusetts, 1975). 1980

Konz, Leo Edwin. **The International Transfer of Commerical Technology** (Doctoral Dissertation, The University of Texas at Austin, 1976) 1980

Logar, Cyril M. **Location of Responsibility for Product-Policy Decisions of United States-Based Multinational Firms Manufacturing Consumer Goods** (Doctoral Dissertation, Kent State University, 1975). 1980

Macaluso, Donald G. **The Financial Advantage of Multinational Firms During Tight Credit Periods in Host Countries** (Doctoral Dissertation, New York University, 1975). 1980

Mascarenhas, Oswald A.J. **Towards Measuring the Technological Impact of Multinational Corporations in the Less Developed Countries** (Doctoral Dissertation, The University of Pennsylvania, 1976). 1980

Moneef, Ibrahim A. Al-. **Transfer of Management Technology to Developing Nations** (Doctoral Dissertation, Indiana University, 1977). New introduction by Stanton G. Cort. 1980

Moore, E[lwood] S. **American Influence in Canadian Mining.** 1941

Moore, Russell M. **Multinational Corporations and the Regionalization of the Latin American Automotive Industry** (Doctoral Dissertation, Tufts University, 1969). Revised edition. 1980

O'Connor, Walter F. **An Inquiry into the Foreign Tax Burdens of U.S. Based Multinational Corporations** (Doctoral Dissertation, The City University of New York, 1976). 1980

Persaud, Thakoor. **Conflicts between Multinational Corporations and Less Developed Countries** (Doctoral Dissertation, Texas Tech University, 1976). 1980

Przeworski, Joanne Fox. **The Decline of the Copper Industry in Chile and the Entrance of North American Capital** (Doctoral Dissertation, Washington University, 1978). 1980

Raveed, Sion. **Joint Ventures between U.S. Multinational Firms and Host Governments in Selected Developing Countries** (Doctoral Dissertation, Indiana University, 1976). 1980

Renforth, William, and Sion Raveed. **A Comparative Study of Multinational Corporation Joint International Business Ventures with Family Firm or Non-Family Firm Partners** (Doctoral Dissertation, Indiana University, 1974). Revised edition. 1980

Siddiqi, M. M. Shahid. **Planning and Control of Multinational Marketing Strategy** (Doctoral Dissertation, The University of Pennsylvania, 1976). 1980

Sorey, Gordon Kent. **The Foreign Policy of a Multinational Enterprise** (Doctoral Dissertation, The University of California, Irvine, 1976). 1980

Stanford Research Institute. **Foreign Investment.** 1980

Stopford, John M. **Growth and Organizational Change in the Multinational Firm** (Doctoral Dissertation, Harvard University, 1968). 1980

Toyne, Brian. **Host Country Managers of Multinational Firms** (Doctoral Dissertation, Georgia State University, 1975). 1980

Tsurumi, Yoshihiro. **Technology Transfer and Foreign Trade** (Doctoral Dissertation, Harvard University, 1968). Revised edition. 1980

Wells, Louis T., Jr. **Product Innovation and Directions of International Trade** (Doctoral Dissertation, Harvard University, 1966). 1980